ADVANCE PRAISE

"Sharon is big-hearted, funny, and my kind of gal. You're going to love her."

–KRISTIN CHENOWETH, Tony and Emmy Award–winning singer and actor

"A warm and enchanting road trip about love, fear, life, and the challenges of changing out a propane tank? Sharon Wheatley's vivid spirit guides us through the American pandemic with courage and a light heart."

–THERESA REBECK, playwright, television writer, and novelist

"Sharon Wheatley takes us on a wild journey through her Broadway life, her second marriage, the death of her parents, a cross-country RV ride, and so much more with warmth, humility, her trademark humor, and flat-out good writing. You'll want to finish it in one sitting."

–SETH RUDETSKY, musician, actor, writer, and celebrated host on Sirius/XM Satelite Radio's *On Broadway*

"Sharon's story reminds us that so much life can happen when you're somewhere in the middle of nowhere—and she and her wonderful family are great companions for the ride. So glad we were invited along for this beautiful story of getting through one of the darkest times with wit, wisdom, and warmth. Equal parts heartbreaking and hilarious, *Drive* proves Sharon is just as talented and entertaining on the page as she is onstage."

–IRENE SANKOFF AND DAVID HEIN, writers of the Tony Award–winning Broadway hit, *Come From Away*

"This book is like a public service to anyone who doesn't have a friend they periodically need to sit down on the couch with just to hear talk—because they're funny, sure, but also because they're mischievously warm and decidedly not aggressive (relaxing, even), and because they're so comfortable with their voice . . . and with you. You know you're in good hands with this person, so you make them coffee and selfishly demand they *just talk* to you, because you know you'll feel safe, and amused, and moved, and ultimately taken care of as her audience of one. If you don't have a friend like this (and even if you do), I'm pleased to announce you can now have Sharon Wheatley and her wonderful recollections all to yourself to make you feel like 1. someone likes you enough to take this uniquely familiar, cozy tone with you and 2. that somehow, even the hardest things in life aren't things you can't (or won't) get through."

—**BD WONG,** Tony Award–winning actor, writer, and director

*thank you for
supporting
live theater.*

DRIVE

STORIES FROM SOMEWHERE

IN THE MIDDLE OF NOWHERE

SHARON WHEATLEY

RIVER GROVE
BOOKS

This book reflects the author's present recollections of experiences over time. Its story and its text are the author's alone. Some details and characteristics may be changed, some events may be compressed, and some dialogue may be recreated.

Published by River Grove Books
Austin, TX
www.rivergrovebooks.com

Copyright © 2022 Sharon Wheatley

Distributed by River Grove Books

Design and composition by Greenleaf Book Group and Brian Phillips
Cover design by Greenleaf Book Group and Brian Phillips
Cover image copyright Danika Bathgate. Used under license from Shutterstock.com

Publisher's Cataloging-in-Publication data is available.

Print ISBN: 978-1-63299-522-3

eBook ISBN: 978-1-63299-523-0

First Edition

Drive *is dedicated to the people in my life*
who drive me to do my best.

Martha, Charlotte, and Tobi.
Or, as Tobi calls us,
The Family of Love and Wisdom.

Thank you for having grit. Thank you for being game.
Thank you for being hilarious.

"Don't worry. Everything is going to be amazing."
—A magnet on our refrigerator

CONTENTS

A QUICK PREFACE

Allegedly, early on in my relationship with Martha, I promised her we would travel around in an RV someday.

I don't remember saying that.

And I have an annoying habit of remembering everything.

Martha, who defines herself as forgetful, is the most nostalgic person I know. She likes old-fashioned candy like Mary Jane's and Circus Peanuts. If left to her own devices, she'd watch TV through an external antenna (never cable!), with a preference for *Hogan's Heroes* reruns or old westerns like *Shane*. As much as my dad would have disapproved of me marrying a woman, he would have loved watching TV with Martha. They have the same taste in both movies and snacks. When my parents died, I moved many of their things from Cincinnati to our high-rise apartment in Manhattan. Martha understands on a deep level why I had to keep a terrible orange floral couch of theirs, just as I understand her need to keep "old and awesome!" bottles discovered in her grandparents' dirt-floored basement.

Martha's storage unit in upstate New York houses the rest of her grandparents' belongings. In the very first video I have of her, which she shot and sent me with great bravado, she rolls up the garage door of the storage unit and then enthusiastically tours me through the stacks of memories. "A cedar chest full of old coins!" "The lovers' lamp!" She pays for this storage unit "with a check!" Although recently they were transferring to an automated system online, which was "horrifying and sad, but also easier." She often makes the 6½-hour drive to visit her storage unit like other people go to Lake George on vacation. Martha has had this storage unit for twenty-six years.

This storage unit is the cause of great hilarity among her enormous group of friends.

This storage unit made it into our wedding vows.

I remembered the storage unit.

I forgot the RV.

CHAPTER 1

AFRICA, 2001

I've heard many 9/11 stories. Some incredibly tragic, like the woman who lost her sister in the attack at the Pentagon, or the siblings whose dad was flying one of the planes that was hijacked and hit the twin towers. But I've also heard stories about people's resilience. About kindness and community. As an original cast member of *Come From Away*, an award-winning Broadway musical about a group of stranded travelers in the days after 9/11, I am constantly awestruck by the outpouring of emotions at the stage door. My castmates and I thank audience members as they hold our hands and tell us their stories. It sometimes feels like the final act of the show. We do our best to soothe them and listen to what they say. We all have 9/11 stories, and too many are tragic. Mine is far from tragic, but it is unusual. It started a month earlier.

On Saturday, August 11th, I was sitting in my apartment in New York City on W. 56th Street, my three-and-a-half-year-old, Charlotte, asleep in her little toddler bed. The phone rang. The time was 11:30 p.m.

"Sharon?" It was my mother, and she was crying. Hard. I could barely understand her, but she said something about the house being on fire and then she screamed something about my dad and a car. And then she hung up. Click. Dial tone.

So now I'm in New York—holding a phone with a dial tone—scared to death that I had just spoken to my mother for the last time. I called back. No one picked up. I called my sister's number and my brother's number. No answer. My parents lived in Cincinnati, Ohio, 638 miles away. I sat and held the phone for an hour, not moving. Barely breathing.

Finally, my phone rang again. It was my mother. Laughing.

"We had *all* the fire trucks here. They had to block off the street!" She was giddy with excitement.

My mother had a weird fascination with sirens. When I was a kid, she used to try to follow the fire trucks to their destination. On August 11th, *she* was their destination, and according to all accounts later, there was a giant line of trucks up and down their street, lights blazing. Just to clarify: this is not like other people who have a fascination with the fire *men*. My mother liked the trucks. With sirens. Which made her kind of like a four-year-old boy.

I wasn't terribly interested in her fire truck fascination right at that moment, instead demanding to know what was happening with my dad and the car. Mom put him on the phone, and he was laughing, too.

"Hiya, darlin'. We've had a little excitement here tonight."

I asked about the car, and he told me he'd run into the burning garage to save it.

"I started it right up and backed it out!"

Some people run into burning buildings to save children; my dad ran into a burning building to save his beloved 1993 candy apple red Cadillac with a soft top and butter leather interior.

"I love that car," he told me in a serious voice.

His car drove me crazy. It only had two doors, which meant any time I visited it made maneuvering Charlotte's car seat in and out back-breaking work. The back seat was full of golf balls and sunglasses. But I was glad he hadn't burned alive trying to save it.

"Charles Wheatley. Could you *please* tell me what happened? Or hand the phone to someone who will!"

I finally got the whole story out of my sister, Susan. She's the sensible one. She's an attorney. Responsibly, she lived one mile away from my parents and dealt with all the things. Like whatever crazy situation my parents were in right now.

"Hello," she said, sort of laughing, more exasperated.

"I hear the Cadillac is fine," I said. "Otherwise, I don't know much."

"Yes, it's too bad that car made it, but the house is trashed."

"What happened?" I was desperate to hear a cohesive narrative. Susan gave it to me.

My parents had gone to see a movie, and came out to a severe lightning storm, or as my dad would describe it, *A hell of a storm!* They'd rushed to the car and driven home. My mother wanted to go to bed when they got home, but my dad, concerned about tornados, said they should go to the basement to play pool.

"As if they've ever played pool?" my sister interjected.

"Right?" I agreed. "I thought the pool table was just for wrapping Christmas presents."

She went on. Just as my father racked up the balls and my mother complained that she hated to play pool and wanted to go to bed, there was a house-rattling lightning strike. The power went out.

My dad thought it was a transformer. My mom, who could never sit still, wanted to see what was going on. Halfway up the stairs she yelled down, "Chuck, it smells like smoke up here." They ran around the pitch-black house until they found the source; the house was on fire above the garage where the electric came in. It wasn't a transformer that was hit, it was their house.

My dad yelled for my mom to get out and they stood in the pouring rain and lightning, watching their house burn. That's when she'd called me, hysterical, watching my dad run into the burning garage to save his car. Then she'd hung up.

Despite every fire truck in Anderson Township showing up, the house sustained a lot of damage. It was clear they weren't going to live there for a long time. When I asked Susan how they were, she said, "Any normal person would be upset. Those two just take it in stride."

My parents stayed at Susan's house overnight and went to a family party the next day. They walked in still smelling of smoke, but excited to tell everyone what had happened, which they did in breathless detail. My mom told my brother, Buzz, "I went in to get some clothes and couldn't see a thing. When I said it was too dark, a fireman handed me a flashlight through the wall. There's a giant hole where the TV used to be!" Buzz told me all of this later, also describing how my mom wrapped up food in napkins, telling everyone "We'll need this for later since we don't have a kitchen anymore." They always walked into a party with an urgent situation. Maybe they'd blown a tire on the way, or my dad's blood sugar was going low, and he needed orange juice immediately. But the fire was the story to end all stories.

◆ ◆ ◆

At first, they went to a suites hotel that had two rooms with a kitchenette and a breakfast buffet, which is fun for two nights, but the word from the insurance company was that they'd be out of their house for four months. I was happy to help. As an actor who toured a lot, I was good at finding temporary housing. I made some calls and secured them a corporate apartment with three bedrooms, all covered by the insurance company. It was a far cry from their large house, but at least it had the essential: a full kitchen. My Dad deemed it "small and claustrophobic" but "livable and better than the hotel." My mother, on the other hand, would have stayed in the hotel, happy with the free coffee and someone making her bed every day.

But there was another issue of greater importance on deck.

My parents had planned and saved for a safari in Africa, and they were set to leave soon after the fire. Even before the fire, the idea of this trip blew me and Susan and Buzz away. My parents rarely traveled, and never traveled together. And now to jet off to Africa? Bananas. It made sense for my dad—he'd gone once many years before—but my mother was afraid of almost everything Africa had to offer: snakes, birds, and most mammals, predatory or not. She wanted a trip with delicious food and drink and nightlife, like Italy. My dad said, "Darlin', there's all the nightlife in the world in Africa, and I want to show it to you." She said she'd go if she could see a giraffe, which he promised her, and they took their savings (with a lot going on a credit card) and booked the trip.

Now, because of the fire, there was a question about whether they should go, and my mom particularly worried about the non-refundable money. But Dad was adamant. "Why reschedule? Hell, there's no better time to go! This'll be the adventure of our lives!" His reasoning was sound. There wasn't much they could do during the demolition, and they'd be back in time to make the renovation decisions. It was settled, they were going. We were happy for them.

◆ ◆ ◆

Mom and Dad flew via Brussels and landed in Nairobi on a Sunday. They had a fun day of hanging around the famous Stanley Hotel while waiting to meet up with the rest of the group to leave on the scheduled safari stops. Mom talked about the dinner they ate that night at a restaurant called Carnivore and the waiters, called "Carvers," walked around with grilled meat on sticks. "Elk and zebra legs—the whole leg!" My mother couldn't even eat chicken off the bone, so I can imagine this was not the meal of her dreams. She told me later, "I told them I was a vegetarian and only ate salad. Your father ate it all. With mayonnaise. I couldn't even look at him."

My Dad said, "Hell of a meal." He loved to eat more than anything in the world.

The next morning, on their first full day, they met up with their small group, six Americans from the West Coast. Mom and Dad had their own tour guide, Abraham, who was assigned to them for the entire trip and in charge of their schedule and general well-being.

They traveled 2-3 hours by car to Sweetwaters Tented Camp, which is a private conservancy that has its own wildlife roaming the grounds. The big event at Sweetwaters is the night safari, which is basically where you climb into a Land Rover with big flashlights and yell, "Here, kitty, kitty, kitty."

Before leaving, they gathered for dinner. Mom and Dad arrived at the main building, which housed the front desk/business office and restaurant, but it was empty. Everyone was crowded into a small bar, watching the TV. My parents rushed in and watched as the twin towers smoked and then fell. Their group stayed at the TV and watched for hours.

On the other side of the world, I was in Atlanta, Georgia, doing *The Phantom of the Opera* in the famous Fox Theater. I'd joined the National Touring Company for a few weeks to cover a vacation, and Charlotte and her dad were visiting. They were supposed to fly back to New York City that morning, and my mother knew that. She was out of her mind with worry and could not reach anyone via phone. She finally managed to send an email from the business office at the camp outside Nairobi, praying someone would read it and write her back. My mother demanded to go home, but my dad said, "Honey, we can't get anywhere right now. The best thing we can do is stay here and do this safari. It's the thrill of a lifetime."

"It's the thrill of your lifetime," she shot back. "I wanted to go to Rome."

When they returned from the night safari, the staff of their hotel ran out with an email back from us, saying we were safe. This calmed my mom down a bit. That, and the fact that because of all the airport closures they actually *couldn't* leave Africa. The domestic flights opened after a few days on a limited basis, but international flights took much longer to start back up. They had no choice but to trust Abraham, their guide, and stay on the trip for the duration.

My parents were very moved by their treatment in Africa. They told us later, "People everywhere apologized to us. They sought out any American on the trip and made sure we knew how sorry they were and how furious they were about the attack. Especially apologetic and protective was Abraham, who was Muslim. He told us over and over again, 'We are not all like this. These are bad, bad men.'" It turned out Abraham's cousins had been killed in the attack by Al Qaeda on the US Embassy in Nairobi.

The sorrow of that time was awful for everyone, but as a mom, I was especially worried about sensitive little Charlotte. My cousin Polly lived in Atlanta, and I went directly to her house the morning of 9/11. We watched the towers fall on her small kitchen TV, trying to shield our young kids from the trauma of that day as they played in the next room. I worked hard to make sure Charlotte knew her JoJo and Poppy were okay and coming back from Africa. Just as urgent, I never wanted her to see the footage of the planes going into the towers. We lived in the middle of New York City, surrounded by tall buildings, and we flew on a lot of airplanes.

And then there was the issue of New York City in the days after 9/11. As we finished up our run of *Phantom* in Atlanta, I didn't want to take Charlotte back to the palpable anxiety in New York. There were fighter planes flying overhead. Our iconic twin buildings were gone. The skyline looked like it had had teeth pulled. Just huge holes. Huge, smoking holes. *Phantom* closed in Atlanta and, as a stroke of luck, was heading to Cincinnati, Ohio, for their next stop. A friend in the cast was driving there, and me and Charlotte hitched a ride, staying in the three-bedroom I'd secured for my parents the week earlier.

We arrived in Cincinnati, and I met Buzz and Mayday, his wife and my best friend well before she ever married Buzz, and their baby daughter Gwendolyn. It was such a relief to be home and with family. International flights were starting back up, but there was a huge wait. My parents didn't even know Charlotte and I were in Cincinnati, let alone in their apartment.

I didn't know how long I'd stay in Cincinnati, but I decided it was best for Charlotte to have something fun to do. I called around and found a preschool that would take her. That day. Just like that. In New York City you have to interview and beg and get letters of recommendation from Oprah and sign a contract in blood if they deem you worthy, but Knox Presbyterian Nursery School said, "Oh, you're from New York and you don't know how long you'll be here? That's fine, bring her on over. Today!" Anytime people found out we were strays from New York City they were exceptionally gracious. The world mourned with us. Cincinnati is not just my hometown, but it's a great town. It's easy. Much easier than the life I lived in New York City with a toddler. In times of upset, Cincinnati is always a good idea.

Later that week, my parents finally made it home. My entire family waited for them with signs and balloons at the newly constructed security gate. They cried when they saw us all there, especially surprised by me and cute Charlotte who'd bought a Santa suit for the occasion and jumped out from behind a partition, running to my mom. They were full of stories about flying and the new security, but mostly they talked about how kind everyone was in Africa. How people apologized when they saw they were Americans, how sad the world was for us. My parents did not have the trip they were expecting, but they had the trip of their lives.

Often when I am performing in *Come From Away*, I think about my mom and dad, who were also stranded international travelers in the days after 9/11. They, like the characters in the show, were waiting for their chance to use a computer to email us to say they were safe, watching the TVs and hoping their flight would eventually be allowed to land back in the United States. Instead of drinking screech and eating toutons like the *Come From Away* characters in Newfoundland, my parents were eating zebra and somewhere out on a jeep with Abraham. I can just picture them, my dad snapping pictures of okapi and taking full advantage of this unexpected adventure, while my mom sits wringing her hands, desperate to come home, but so grateful for the kindness of strangers.

CHAPTER 2

MIRACLES

I got the call that I'd been cast in *Come From Away* as my mother got word that her cancer was terminal. I don't mean around the same time, or on the same day. I mean at the same time. She was in the hospital in Cincinnati, and I was with her, having flown in from San Diego.

My family and I had moved to San Diego a few years earlier, in 2013, wanting a new life, a new career, a dishwasher, a golden retriever, and an overall happier state of being. I was desperate for it. After over twenty years of nearly steady work, my acting career was at a standstill. Auditions became depressing. Directors constantly told me I was "talented" but also "not the right type." I'd started writing some shows, writing blogs for profit, and had dreams of a career in TV writing and some sunny weather. I left behind my entire acting career, consoling myself that four shows on Broadway was pretty good. I told myself, "I'm out. That's it." As I watched the New York City skyline disappear in my rear-view mirror, I stifled any voice in me that still had acting ambition. *You had a great career.* Now I was choosing my family. And truthfully, things had slowed down. As a woman of a certain age and at a certain weight, the job opportunities were fewer and fewer, the rejection overwhelming. It was easy to justify leaving.

Only one thing haunted me: I'd never had an original role on Broadway. So much comes with it if you're lucky: the Tony Awards, the honor of recording the original cast album, the Macy's Day Parade, and basically every single thing you dream about if you are thirteen-year-old Sharon Wheatley in her bedroom in Cincinnati, Ohio, singing along to *Annie*. My mom would walk by my closed door as she was on her way to the pool, and I could tell when her Dr. Scholl's stopped flipping that she'd stopped to listen. "I know you're listening at the door!" I'd yell to her, and wait to hear the flip, flop continue down the hall.

I loved that she loved it, but being 13, I was still a brat.

When we got to San Diego, I hung up my jazz shoes and poured myself into trying to make it as a television writer. I spent a few years writing scripts in my San Diego garage and when I had something to show for it, I "took" meetings in LA. I know a lot of LA slang. That's mostly what I got out of my time in LA. I'll circle back to you if I think of anything else and your people can set up a lunch with my people so I can tell you all about it.

My mother, who had always loved my Broadway career almost as much as I did, never wanted me to move to San Diego. She was unrelenting. "You belong in New York," she told me, time and time again. "You are supposed to be on stage." It made me bananas. My mom loved everything I did. She watched from the side bragging and cheering me on. This was a rare moment of discord with my mom, and it was unsettling. I did everything I could to avoid her advice, stopping short of plugging my ears up and singing the *Star-Spangled Banner* to drown her out. I was going to San Diego and nothing was going to stop me. I was out.

Just before we moved, I found out about my mom's initial cancer diagnosis. Moving thousands of miles away from her was meant to prove my confidence in the diagnosis that one surgery would fix it all. Medical science overrode any nagging emotional voice in my head. *She's fine. The doctors say this is a routine surgery.* I figured it was just a little farther than New York, which was a twelve-hour drive or a two-hour flight. Once you're on a plane, who cares if it's an hour or six hours. You can make it in a day, I reasoned.

We'd heard different things at different points in her illness. At first the initial surgery would fix it. Then they said there would be occasional surgeries to remove blockages caused by scarring. We'd heard it was a chronic illness and not terminal. We'd heard a monthly shot would keep the tumors at bay. We'd heard she needed a new diet, a new specialist, a new probiotic. But the reality was different. She had more and more pain, numerous trips to the ER, and hospital stays that went from "just overnight" to two weeks nearly every time. On better days, when she could leave the house, she carried an extra set of clothes in addition to wearing two adult diapers because she could not control her bowels. She somehow dragged herself to work for several more years, where she worked as an administrative assistant for the very doctors who were treating her. They would sometimes admit her to the hospital straight from her desk.

I can't count the number of times I got a call from her, crying in her car, because she hadn't made it to the bathroom in a public place or at work. Even when they re-routed her bowels to an ostomy bag, she could not manage it and it would explode.

She started to smell all the time, which she found mortifying. She was what my kids would call a "girlie-girl"—always in makeup with beautifully manicured nails and a closet full of nice clothes and racks of shoes and bags. She especially prided herself on smelling good, using light layers of lotions and perfumes to create a signature scent. People constantly commented, "Mary Jo, you always smell great!"

When I was little, I used to read books in her closet, comforted by the lingering scent of her. But now, I worried my kids would forever associate the bathroom smell with my mother.

My mom still managed to travel, a real testament to her grit. She'd pack up my dad, who by now had become a colossal pain in the ass to travel with for numerous reasons, including but not limited to: he couldn't walk well, he had dementia, and he needed constant monitoring for his diabetes, something he thought was "overkill."

As feeble as she was, she put him in a wheelchair, pushed him to the gate, shot him up with insulin, and flew to San Diego. I couldn't wait for them to arrive; I was thrilled and so proud to show off the life we'd created. The first time she visited she got off the plane, looked around, and said, "It's so brown." San Diego was not her thing, and *me* in San Diego made her very unhappy. Cute house, sunshine, the ocean, fish tacos. Everyone loves San Diego. What was her problem?

She felt like shit. That was her problem. And she wanted me closer to her and back on Broadway.

The fact was, she was right. Living so far away from her proved to be torturous. There was no direct flight from San Diego to Cincinnati, and the flights were expensive. The three-hour time difference made the timing of phone calls difficult. There was also just, I don't know, so much *space* between us. So many miles. I felt as far from her as I was, and in New York I'd somehow still felt close to home.

Still, as her cancer progressed, I flew home often, staying in the house with my dad. This helped ease the burden on my sister and brother, who lived in town and handled a crushing amount of work in the care of my parents. As awful as it all was, I count these quiet hospital days as some of my closest times with my mom. I got into a routine where I would stay up late talking to my dad, teasing him about his horrible TV shows, get up in the morning, give him his insulin shot, and then drive over to the hospital, where I would stay for ten-hour stretches with Mom. She would sleep off and on, waking up to talk a little to me or the nurse. Sometimes I would look up and see her awake, staring off into space.

"What are you doing?" I'd ask.

"Praying for a miracle," she'd respond.

"You've got this, Mama. You're doing great. This is just a hiccup."

Her response was always the same. "I hate this."

We worried about her mental state. Cheering Mom up was a full-time job. I told stories about the kids, I combed her hair, I made her put on lipstick. My sister and I took turns finding any food she loved and bringing it to her, just to have her take a small bite and push it aside. We'd try something else. Maybe ice cream. The special cream horn from the bakery she'd always loved.

Anything to make her happy.

Nothing made her happy.

She wanted a miracle.

◆ ◆ ◆

On one of my trips to Cincinnati, I got a Facebook message out of the blue from a casting director I knew quite well in New York asking if I was available or interested in auditioning for a brand-new show called *Come From Away* at the La Jolla Playhouse, an excellent theater in San Diego. Her message caught me totally off guard. When you leave show business it feels like you've stepped into quicksand, like the ground swallows you up and no one ever remembers you were there. But Rachel Hoffman at Bernie Telsey Casting remembered.

In the message she asked, "What are you doing in San Diego?"

The voice in my head answered her loudly.

What AM I doing in San Diego?

Was I a writer? A mother? A daughter? Was any of this enough without also performing? Was I interested in pursuing performing at all these days? I had left the business for a reason. Broadway can be a brutal ride. Despite doing major hits (ask an actor any question and you'll get their resume) like *Les Miserables, The Phantom of the Opera, Cats*, and *Avenue Q*, I'd had my pure love of theater shamed out of me quickly. My very first night performing on Broadway I was doing *Les Miserables* and in one scene, we had to run in slow-motion, away from a runaway cart. The theater trick here is simple, just slow-motion running on a turntable with special lighting, but it is effective and really cool. Very much the kind of thing I might have practiced for hours in my bedroom as a kid. As I was running in slow-mo and feeling the runaway cart nipping at my heels that first night, I was ecstatic. I'd made it! I was on Broadway! Years of work, hope, and dedication propelled me forward, and I was welcomed into this troop of like-minded talent. If I died it would say on my tombstone *"She made it to Broadway."* As this was all happening, a guy sped up his slow-mo and ran next to me and spoke aloud.

"Hey, Sharon. Calm down, it's just a play." And then he'd laughed an awful, patronizing laugh.

The thirteen-year-old in me screamed in pain, a tiny death. Over and over again, for years, I endured both ends of Broadway, the thrill of success and the reality of the cynicism that comes from doing eight shows a week in a job you've grown tired of. I learned to silence my enthusiasm. It simply wasn't cool.

When I got the message on Facebook about *Come From Away*, something old inside me lit up. I had to share the news with the person I knew would be the most delighted. The one in the Dr. Scholl's who listened at the door.

I went to my mom and woke her up.

"Mom. Listen to this."

I read her the message. My mom had this very cute habit of raising her eyebrows quickly when something piqued her interest. Her eyebrows shot up as she looked at me, her thin hands resting on her chin. Before she said a word, I knew I was going to audition. My mom was the best kind of stage mother. She didn't ever push me, but she knew what I wanted before I did. She needed this. We needed this.

I smiled at her. "Do you think I can still sing? It's been a while."

"I love when you sing."

It was decided.

I wrote Rachel back, got the audition materials, and started working on my audition in Mom's hospital room. When she was alert enough, she'd run lines with me. Sometimes she was too sick to do anything but lie there and listen to me work on the songs. She'd weigh in with her eyes closed. "This is heaven."

So, I sang more, all for my mom. I am not a person who naturally sings in front of a small group of people; I get very embarrassed. I am better on a stage, which gives me some separation. I did occasionally agree to sing for people—I'd recently sung to the ward of nurses in my mom's hospital. This wasn't my idea. My sister told the nurses I was a Broadway singer, so when I asked if my mom could have a room with a window in the ICU, they bribed me, saying they'd move her if I sang for them. My mom knew I hated singing in front of people in a small group like that—I'd refused it for years when she'd beg me to sing for her bridge group or at a family reunion—but this was all about getting my mom, who was miserable, a window with a view. So I ponied up. I asked the nurses what they'd like to hear and finally settled on a song from *The Little Mermaid*. The nurses liked it, but Dad, who was also in the room, said it was "too mansy-pansy," and wanted another song. "Come on, you've got more than that. Really belt one out."

As if I could jump up on the nurses' desk like Liza Minnelli and pump my arms in a sequined outfit. My dad saw no issue with this. My mom kept her eyes closed but waved her hand in an ixnay way. I didn't belt out another one, but my mom got her view.

After the doctors released my mom from the hospital I went back to San Diego, well-rehearsed and ready for my audition thanks to the many hours in my hospital rehearsal room. I called my mom from the parking lot of the La Jolla Playhouse, the renowned theater company who was producing the show, and said, "Okay. I'm here. Wish me luck."

"Call me as soon as you are done."

I was nervous.

I walked into the audition room, Seuss One, named after the one and only Doctor who had donated money to the theater, and waited for the assistant to call my name. I tried to be jaded and nonchalant, but I was excited despite myself. I'd read the script and had that deep feeling, deeper than my anxiety, the calm when you know this project is special, and even better, that I might be right for it.

They called me in for the role of Beulah, a character who ran the Gander Academy, and for the audition I had to tell a joke she tells in the show and sing part of a song. I knew in my heart I would not get this job. I am a terrible joke teller. The worst. But the show was so good that I had to try. I figured I might be an understudy.

Knowing I had a shot made me vulnerable. Show business is painful. It's all about getting your hopes up repeatedly, then being led along and dumped in the end, just to stand up and start over again. It's hard on my heart. My friend Brynn puts it best. "Show business is like an abusive boyfriend. He knocks you around, promises you he won't do it again, and just when you trust him, he punches you in the gut."

I walked into the audition with my heart open, fully knowing I could get gut-punched. I tried to not care as much as I could by refusing to iron my shirt. If I pulled out an iron it felt like I was trying too hard. I went wrinkled. Take *that*, showbiz.

In the waiting room sat excited people dressed in attractive, well-ironed clothes. I did wonder, as I looked at the women in high heels and suits, if they'd read the same script I had. Maybe I was wrong to dress in leggings and boots and a fisherman's sweater. It was about an island in Newfoundland, right?

Chris Ashley, the artistic director of the La Jolla Playhouse and the director of *Come From Away*, was in the room with one other person who was running a camera. They were filming it for all the other writers and creative team who did not attend these waste-of-time auditions, knowing (as I did) the "real" auditions would occur in New York City. The camera reminded me, *Don't get excited. These are fake auditions. They say they are looking for "local" talent. They aren't. It's probably already cast.* The abusive boyfriend was asking to rekindle the flame. I felt the lure.

I did what I was asked to do. I told the joke. I sang the songs. It felt good to perform, even though I was in an audition room and not on a stage. Then Chris Ashley, whom I'd only heard of because he was, you know, a pretty famous Broadway director, said, "Do you want to sing something else? Did you bring something?"

I had brought something of my own, a song from a long-lost musical called *The Baker's Wife*, written by Stephen Schwartz, best known as the composer of *Wicked*. As I sang, I felt a release in me. Like I was thirteen again, up in my bedroom, singing for the pure joy of singing. Full of hope, full of the sense that I was doing exactly what I was supposed to do. It was a rare reconnection with my younger self.

Something rekindled. Somehow the break away from the business, the move from New York, something with my mom—I don't know. But I broke open that day. I found my love again.

I remember exactly what Chris said to me when I finished. "So, you live here in San Diego?"

"Yes," I replied.

He looked surprised. "Aren't we lucky."

I called Mom immediately and told her the whole thing. She could not have said *I told you so* in more ways. I told her Chris had said they were lucky to find me. My mom's response was simple: "They were."

I received a callback, and they switched the role from Beulah to Diane, the Texan whose primary job is to make the ultimate decision to, as she says, "Be whoever I want to be." I put my final audition on video, uploaded it, and sent it off to be looked at in New York. Now my job was simply "to wait." It was agonizing. I knew I was going up against the best of the best in New York City. I tried to stop thinking about it. I tried to tell myself it was okay no matter what. I reminded myself I don't ever get to do new shows and I am almost always an understudy. I reminded myself just *how* abusive that show business boyfriend could be.

In the meantime, I flew back to Cincinnati to accept an alumni award at my high school. Hours after I got home, a Thursday, I found my mom crumpled on the steps, weeping. There was something terribly wrong. I took her to the hospital, and they checked her in, all of us hoping it was nothing more than dehydration. Since my award presentation also lined up with me doing a full-blown concert, my mother was bound and determined to be out of the hospital for the

Saturday night concert. She told the nurses and doctors, "I have to be out by Saturday."

On Friday, she went in for a round of tests and I was with her, barely remembering that today was casting day for *Come From Away*. As the day ticked later and later, we waited for the oncology team to stop by my mom's room with the results of her tests. Late in the afternoon, my cell phone rang. Mom was sleeping, so I took the call out in the hallway, a small solarium with a soda machine and vinyl chairs.

It was my agent, Craig.

"Hiya, gorgeous."

A loud announcement from the nurses' station blasted through the speakers, and Craig heard it.

"Am I catching you at a bad time? Where are you?"

"I'm in the hospital with my mom. It's okay, she's asleep and I am out of the room."

We talked about my mom for a minute and then he said, "I have some great news. You are being offered the role of Diane in *Come From Away*."

I was silent. Shocked. Surely, I had not won out over all the people in New York.

I had to clarify.

"Am I the understudy?"

Craig laughed. "No. You are it. You are being offered the role of Diane."

He went on to say all kinds of things like *I told you so* and *I always knew you had the best ahead of you, even when you said you were quitting the business*, and other things I could barely hear because I was so in shock. My little thirteen-year-old self started to cheer inside. I could feel the excitement.

Then I saw a team of doctors walk out of my mom's room.

"Craig, I have to go. I'll call you back."

When I walked back into my mom's room, she was crying.

"They can't do anything, Sharon. They are saying they can't do anything."

She told me what they said, which was everything we didn't want to hear. It had spread. They could not control it. It was a matter of time. We cried. I held her. I asked questions. After a while, I thought about my phone call, and I wondered what to do with this news.

I have another friend who recently died of cancer, and he started every conversation with "Tell me something good." The need for good news, any news, something that wasn't "you're dying," was palpable.

I noticed she'd sunk down in her bed, and I grabbed her by both armpits and hoisted her up. Then I said, "I have some good news. Do you want to hear it?" In cartoons they do the animation where they make the tears fly straight out of their eyes rather than rolling down their cheeks, and that's what my mom's tears looked like when I broke the news about *Come From Away*. In a moment of complete despair, of the undisputed worst news, *Come From Away* delivered its first gift to me and my mother. Happiness.

We set new goals: "You'll get better and come see the show!" We dreamed the show would go to Broadway. That I would be in the Macy's Day Parade. My mother held onto my young dreams with a ferocity that surprised me. Even when I'd given up on me, my mother hadn't. She did not make it to the concert at my school the next day, but I got ready in her hospital room, and we managed to have her listen in on FaceTime. I could hear the beeps of her monitors as I sang in front of the crowd. I had the entire audience yell, "Get better, Mary Jo!"

Mom never saw *Come From Away* in person. However, near the end of the run in La Jolla, my stage manager, Martha, who knew what was happening and how sad I was that my mom was missing the show, gave me a video of the show, something we never get. This was filmed to use as "archival video" to be used later to train our understudies.

"It's not a great video," she explained, "and please don't mention that I gave it to you. But I thought it might be nice for your mom to see it."

Martha's parents were also ill, something we'd discovered early on in rehearsals when I'd given her a heads-up to make sure there was an understudy for me. "Hopefully, I will not need an understudy. But if I must go, I will go." Martha and I started to talk about sick parents and compare notes on how to be a good daughter as she and I became friends. There is something so kismet about Martha, who never met my mother, making a way for my mom to see me in *Come From Away*. Mom watched it in one sitting, on my computer, with tubes all over her. I worried she would not know who I was. I worried it would not translate to screen. I watched her watch it, marveling that she could sit up for so long.

When it was over, she looked at me, tears streaming down her face, and said, "It's beautiful. So beautiful. I hope it goes to Broadway. You deserve it."

Come From Away did go on to Broadway. I recorded the original cast album. I was on the Tony Awards. Chris Ashley won the Tony Award for best director. The cast is beautiful, positive, and happy to be at work every day. We even filmed the show as more than an archival video. We made it into a movie.

Martha became my wife.

I now live in New York again.

My mother missed all of it.

CHAPTER 3

THE SHUTDOWN

At the time of the Covid-19 shutdown I was set to perform my 1,283rd performance in *Come From Away*. I'd been with the show since April of 2015 and after performing six days a week for so many years, my job was solid; I had what people in my business call "a government job" with excellent healthcare, regular donations to a pension and 401K, and enough money to cover all my family's expenses and then some. I'd ordered an extravagant Peloton bike. I was, as my dad would have said, Living the Dream, Kid.

Martha was working on another show on Broadway, *Diana*, a giant and glitzy musical about the life and legacy of Princess Diana of Wales. With Martha and me working, and my youngest child, Tobi, in an intensely difficult school, our lives had been chaotic by most measures for those first few months of 2020. For months Martha and I had seen each other only in passing. I got up early to drive Tobi to school, Martha was gone by the time I got back, and we both came home late. We were still newlyweds enough to complain about missing time with each other, so we'd forgo sleep and stay up for hours when she got home trying to catch up on our days before we passed out. Martha is the Production Stage Manager and to that end she manages basically everyone in the building and oversees all things that have to do with the running of the show. Her show was "in previews," which are the performances leading up to the opening night performance and party where everyone dresses up in their red carpet best and drinks like fish until the review comes in from the *New York Times*. During the preview performance time there are long and arduous rehearsals during the day where new songs and scenes are tried out as everyone tries to fine-tune the show, leaving all parties involved completely and totally wasted and anxious. No one can afford a bad review in the *Times*, which will shutter a show almost as fast as a global pandemic.

I did everything I could to make things easy at home and to keep my focus more on my sixth grader and less on household chores. Even while at work I would manage things at home via phone and text. Then once the curtain came down, I'd fly through the autograph line at the stage door to take selfies and sign autographs as fast as I could, in order to race home to tuck Tobi into bed. Then we'd wake up at 6:20 am to start the day all over again. It was hard but it was working. We were happy. I'm not one to let good times pass me by, so I'd often remind Tobi and Martha to stop and say thanks for all of our good fortune. I'd had enough crappy times in the near past to know when to celebrate the present.

The first time I registered the fear of the growing infection in China was in late January 2020. I was hosting a 12th-birthday party for Tobi and their friend Steph. (Important note: Tobi is non-binary and goes by they/them pronouns. Yes, this might be confusing at first. But trust me when I say: A) You'll get used to it. B) It was harder for me than you. And C) it's all okay and not weird. This is a happy kid, which is all that matters.)

I knew little Steph was a worrier, and that she was nervous during the first part of the party, which was an Escape Room set in a bakery. Basically, you had to figure out how to make a bunch of cupcakes—nothing stressful, just fun. We weren't saving the world from the Nazis, just making cupcakes. But Steph was a mess. She quizzed the person who worked there, asking repeatedly if there would be loud noises, if anyone would jump out to scare us, and how she could escape from the room early. We all took turns soothing her and assuring her everything would be fine, and that figuring out how to *escape* the Escape Room was the point of the game. Steph wasn't having it. The employee showed her numerous times what button to push if she wanted to leave the room early. The employee explained the room was not scary at all; it was a bakery and all we had to do was find the ingredients and make the cupcakes in time. "And then," she explained in a nice tone that did not completely cover her irritation, "if you make it, you get to eat the cupcakes at the end. And you don't even have to worry about that because I'll give you the cupcakes anyway."

Steph still seemed skeptical.

Later, in the Westway Diner where we went to have Tobi's birthday dinner with all their[1] pals, Steph caught sight of the TV playing in the corner. The CNN chyron included the new words Covid-19. Steph looked at me with giant eyes and said, "I am so scared that I will catch Covid-19."

I laughed and said, "You are not going to get Covid-19. We are fine!" I went back to my chicken souvlaki platter.

I still think of her and what I said. Honestly, I am pissed off that her anxiety was right. I wanted her to be able to push the "let me out" button but still get the cupcakes. Poor kid. But I also appreciate her anxiety. I put Steph in the same category as the dogs who can predict earthquakes and start to bark moments before the earthquake

---

1   Reminder: their = just Tobi. You'll get the hang of it.

hits. Steph was my early warning system. I'm not sure I would have taken the virus as seriously without her.

As February became March it seemed all our late-night conversations turned to nothing but the Coronavirus. Broadway has an international audience, and our workplace is the definition of density—just ask anyone who must try to get up and squeeze through the row to use the restroom—so we had some major concerns. Because of her job, Martha often heard more about what was happening in the management conversations and she would catch me up in our late-night pow-wows. "They are saying they might stop performances for a while, but it seems so hard to believe. What would that even look like?"

I am the news-watcher in our relationship, so I was slowly realizing the enormity of the problem as the images and stories of Covid-19 got closer and closer to our lives. I began to quietly compile a collection of things I thought we might need if we were to have to shelter inside. Cleaning products. Gloves. Canned goods. Water. Rice. Toilet paper and paper towels. Sometimes I'd see other people in the grocery store who seemed to be on the same trajectory I was, and we'd nod to each other as we recognized ourselves in our identical shopping carts. The unsaid thing was "I hope we're wrong. I'd be thrilled to be wrong."

Martha, bleary eyed from rehearsals and performances, finally noticed my stockpile when the dining room table was so full of supplies that she could barely sit down to eat her dinner. She didn't really tease me. Instead, she quietly started collecting what she felt was critical: large quantities of pet food.

Now that I had thought my home life through, I turned my attention to work.

I was also worried. The backstage of a Broadway show is, in a word, tight. Take any Hollywood version of what the backstage of a show looks like and erase it. Dressing rooms are cramped. The buildings are, in most cases, historical landmarks in dire need of renovation. The HVAC systems can barely keep the building climate controlled, let alone well ventilated. We are all on top of each other all the time.

Imagine a family of five living in a one-room apartment. Now imagine that family of five doing, let's say, an aerobics class. Now add that the family of five is doing an aerobics class in that one room while also singing at the top of their lungs. That's what Broadway's like.

For example, in *The Phantom of the Opera* at the Majestic Theater, because the dressing rooms were up many, many flights of stairs, we were changing into those elaborate costumes on narrow concrete stairwells, costumes which are choreographed down to the rhinestone earring placement. On that staircase you had six or eight or ten actors all changing from one gigantic costume into another gigantic costume, plus executing a wig change. It can sometimes take three people per actor to pull off a costume change that must happen in a forty-five-second span. There is no room for error. If you were to come backstage anywhere mid-show and put your purse down in the wrong place, it would cause at best a traffic jam, at worst a serious injury.

Additionally, we are a famously huggy and kissy crowd, which is an image you've seen in the movies and that one stands true. I don't think most law firms start the day with everyone hugging and kissing hello, but a Broadway show does. And that is just what happens off stage. On stage there is all kinds of spitting. Have you seen Jonathan Groff sing as the King in *Hamilton*? I need you to see that to really get my point here, so I'll wait while you check it out.

Now that you've seen that spit show, imagine being the little Coronavirus germ seeking a loving host in which to grow and duplicate.

I think you're picking up what I'm putting down. I always joke with Joel Hatch, who plays Mayor Claude, that I watch his shiny spit fly into my eye every night during the big *Screech In* number. Joel is nothing if not consistent, so I can count on taking home a little piece of him show after show. And just in case I don't get some spit from Joel, I also kiss Jim Walton three times per show. Broadway is the opposite of social distancing; it's social "near-ness-ing." The audiences sit side by side, the actors and crew and band are shoulder to shoulder, and you can't just open a window for a cross breeze.

All of the above is true, but so is something else. The show must go on.

I became hypervigilant at work. My knuckles started to bleed from the amount of hand sanitizer I slathered on. I would joke in the wings before I'd make my initial entrance that I was going to start gargling with Purell. As things began to disappear from store shelves, I became concerned that we would run out of supplies backstage. On March 4th I emailed my producers:

Two quick things. Martha mentioned that the actors at "Diana" were asked to use only their own sharpies in the stage door line and not take selfies to limit close contact with the audience groups. I thought I'd pass that along in case that was a consideration for us.

Also, I was wondering if we might have some Lysol provided for all the bathrooms? Especially the heavily trafficked stage level bathroom. There is some stuff in there that smells like "apple"—but I am not sure if it is a cleanser?

An ounce of prevention, I suppose. None of these things seem extreme, just simple preventative measures for a little bit, if you agree.

The cast is calm—no one is talking about this—just so you know. We joke around about it.

I felt crazy. Like I was overreacting. I also thought I possibly was right, as much as I did not want to be. I remember one moment in late February when I called my company manager and asked if there was any proviso for us getting paid should there be a work stoppage due to Covid-19. His hesitation led me to ask if I was the first person to call about this. His response is etched in my brain. "You are the first person who has thought of it." I tried to put it out of my mind.

Everyone has heard the phrase "The Show Must Go On!" and also "Denial Is a River in Egypt." These seemingly unrelated sayings are both part of the same in Broadway world. To make that show go on, eight shows a week, fifty-two weeks a year, a person has to live in a fairly constant state of denial.

Injury: I have a sprained ankle and my doctor said to ice it, elevate it, and use crutches.

Denial: If I tape it up like crazy and take four Advil, I can make it through the show.

Martha calls this phenomenon "Dr. Footlights." Are you sick at home? Come to work and when you step onto that stage in front of an audience all your illnesses will magically improve. That's Dr. Footlights.

Dr. Footlights is sometimes aided by actual medical doctors. The worst example I've ever heard was back when there was a production running on Broadway that shall remain nameless but starred a little kid. The kid lost their voice the night the critic from the *New York Times* was coming to review the show. Everyone freaked out, and the kid, who had been like a machine, carrying a multi-million-dollar Broadway show at the same time they were also learning their multiplication tables for school, was in a white-hot panic. A few hours before the curtain went up, a doctor arrived at the theater, took the child into a dressing room, and gave them steroid shots in each arm. The child came out crying and jacked up on steroids, but able to sing. No one really blinked an eye, including the kid's parents. I'm not throwing shade, we all do it. In the week of the Tony Award nominations, I did *Come From Away* with a concussion and four staples in my head. No one *asked* me to do that. No one would have *wanted* me to do that. But I took it upon myself to underplay what had happened, and I went to work anyway. We're athletes. "Put me back in the game, Coach!" is the same sentiment as "The Show Must Go On!" We do it. And if we really can't do it, the show still goes on because there is an amazing team of standbys and understudies eager to take your place.

But what if everyone is at risk of getting sick at the same time? What happens then?

On March 6th we had an emergency meeting at work where the general managers put new social distancing measures in place (this is before that was a phrase). Similar meetings convened at all the Broadway theaters. No visitors of any kind were allowed backstage, and the entire theater would be cleaned after every performance. The autograph line, often called "Stage dooring," is a popular way for fans to get an up-close-and-personal experience with the stars in their favorite shows. The theater did not cancel the autograph line but gave some guidelines. The actors would 1) avoid touching anyone in line, 2) use hand sanitizer, 3) wear gloves, which would be provided should we want them, and 4) forgo the taking of selfies. I can't speak for anyone else, but personally found all those measures difficult to enforce. The first night I bypassed the autograph line and three people stopped me on the street by grabbing my hand. Numerous people stopped me for a selfie, and I can't count how many hugs I received by a person embracing me while saying, "I know I shouldn't but . . ."

Our show is about kindness. To deny our audiences that kind of contact seemed heartless. And the idea that a global pandemic was a real thing still seemed impossible.

On March 11th, which was a two-show Wednesday, we had a morning rehearsal for *Good Morning America*, the ABC morning show on which we were to perform the following day. As we waited in the holding room to get our microphones, my friend Petrina looked closely at the wallpaper. "Is that design a Covid-19 cell?" We all moved closer to look and sure enough the black and red wallpaper was full of Covid-19 cell graphics. It turns out our holding room was also the Covid-19 "war room" where the nightly briefings by doctors and politicians took place.

We rehearsed the song we were set to perform the next morning and then went back across Times Square to do the first of our two shows. Neither show on March 11th was well attended, which is noticeable for any show, but made more obvious due to the fact that *Come From Away* had played to a sold-out crowd for the entirety of the three years we'd been on Broadway. Maybe we wouldn't notice a few seats empty, but when it's half of the house? It's noticeable. And it was all we talked about before the lights went down. At some point during that day word came that an usher at the theater next door had been diagnosed with Covid-19, prompting the shuttering of that show. My friend Pete, the stage left prop guy with whom I confer on a range of important things, from whether I should have a mint Tic Tac or an orange one to how to best handle planning my retirement, said he'd heard we were shutting down on Friday, that we'd be closed over the weekend, and reopen on Tuesday. To my ears that sounded reasonable. I was hopeful. Surely a deep cleaning would do it.

But hope quickly faded as I walked home. Things were starting to feel somewhat surreal in Manhattan; the grocery store shelves were emptying out and there was a palpable fear in the air. It kind of felt like the night before a giant storm was supposed to hit, but without any of the festive anticipation. People were skittish. That same evening the NBA suspended its season. That sent chills down my spine. We knew something was coming but we did not know what or when or for how long. I went home anxiously thinking I needed to at least try to get some sleep as I had an early call at *Good Morning America* the next day.

At 6:15 a.m. on Thursday, March 12th, I walked back to our Covid-19-wallpapered holding room and met up with everyone to shoot our segment. As we walked back to the theater there was a line of people waiting to buy tickets for our show. Audiences and box offices, as well as all of us, thought the show would go on. A woman stopped me on the street for a selfie, saying, "Do you mind? Just in case there is no show tonight!" I said yes to the picture, but I also laughed to myself and imagined how I would tell my dressing roommate about the woman who thought there might be no show.

I walked home to check on Tobi, who was experiencing their first day of school on Zoom due to a student whose grandparent had tested positive for Covid-19. Martha was already at *Diana* rehearsal, and she sent a message saying she thought a Broadway shutdown was imminent. Not sure what to do, I took a nap. After all, I had a show that night and I'd had very little sleep. When I woke up, the governor was holding a press conference on TV and *that* is how I learned Broadway was shut down, effective immediately. I took a picture of the TV screen, sent it to Martha, and lay back down. March 12th, 2020, was the three-year anniversary of *Come From Away* opening on Broadway, a date now shared with a global pandemic that shut down the entire world.

I realized, despite all my preparation, I had not imagined for even one second that Broadway would shut down long-term. I'd imagined that a shutdown would be for two weeks max, and that's what I'd planned for. A long weekend of being off. We had tickets to see SIX on Sunday night (a Christmas present to my kids), and my older daughter Charlotte had a plane ticket to come in the next day, spend the weekend, see the show with us, and then jet off to New Zealand to see her girlfriend. That was it. That's all I thought might happen. Soup, Scrabble, SIX, Charlotte, and then back to work.

As soon as it was announced that Broadway was shuttering for a month, my phone exploded with people amazed that it had happened. Broadway so rarely goes dark. There have been shutdowns due to hurricanes or blizzards. There is an occasional power outage. The longest shutdowns come from labor disputes (the longest was 25 days in 1975). After the attacks on the World Trade Center, the shows were shut down for only two days. Then the Broadway community was called upon to get back to work, get the economy going, and send the signal that New York City was safe. The first night back, two days after 9/11, casts all across Broadway led the audiences in singing "God Bless America." And in the pandemic of 1918, Broadway did not shut down at all.

I watched the news in amazement. It was really happening. In many ways I was like, okay, I planned for this. Martha is coming home, and we can all rest and relax and feel like we are in the right place. We'll be here. At home in New York City. We've got this.

But one thing was seriously nagging me.

We lived in a forty-six-floor high-rise in Midtown, and on February 25th there was a water main break that flooded the elevator banks. As in knocking them out. All six elevators were initially down, but after inspection they were able to put three of the six back in service. Three of the elevators were seriously damaged and would be out of service for at least two months. It became abundantly clear that living on a high floor might offer us terrific views, but the elevators in our building were *exactly* what we needed to avoid at all costs. We had two dogs who needed walks at least twice a day so sheltering inside and avoiding the elevators was out of the question. No one was wearing a mask. No one was wearing gloves. No one knew they were supposed to. And people continued to pile on the elevators to the point that if you had a sandwich in your backpack, it was smashed by the time you exited the elevator because you were pressed up against the wall so hard.

By Friday, March 13th, as things were really starting to ramp up in the US and the virus was exploding in Europe, the elevator situation really started to tug at me. Was there any possible solution to this? Any way to make things better? Without telling Martha I started to look at Airbnb's in my hometown of Cincinnati.

I didn't think I was serious. But I was also sending messages about whether certain hosts would take pets, and then fielding answers about size and weight of dogs. Martha is often better with a proposal that includes a completed plan rather than having to make decisions. Her entire job is about managing people and she makes so many decisions at work that when she comes home, she doesn't want to make any. I love making decisions, so this is no problem for me.

I hadn't totally decided yet. But I was heavily leaning towards taking one last kamikaze elevator ride to the garage and getting my posse out of there. We were fortunate; I keep a car in the garage of our building. It's the Ohio in me, I always have a car. This car gave us a free pass past all the contagions of travel. No need for public transportation. No need for an airplane or train. We could load that car in a few risky elevator trips and head out at any point. I kept mulling it over in my head. *Why not go to Cincinnati? Tobi would*

love to see their cousin Lizzy. Spring is nice there. There are fewer peo-
ple. You've got a car sitting down in the garage. Just do it. Cincinnati is
always a good idea.

After watching the news Friday morning, I made up my mind. I told Tobi to start to pack their stuff. "Bring everything for school, kid."

Martha was napping. After months of twelve- to sixteen-hour days, she was relieved to finally be at home. When I finally let her in on my thoughts about leaving, she burst into tears.

"I don't want to leave. I have so much to do! Your side of the room is totally clean. I was really looking forward to cleaning up my side of the room! And the mail! And taxes! And what about the pets?"

"We'll take the pets."

"All of them?"

"We're leaving no one behind, Martha. We all go. It's just for two weeks."

That gave her pause. She thought about it.

"Well, okay. That makes me feel better."

I booked a house for two weeks starting the next day. Martha pulled herself together, stood up, hoisted the laundry over her shoulder, and we got to the business of leaving town. I had a refrigerator full of groceries. My pantry was full of flour and baking supplies. I had rolls and rolls of paper towels and toilet paper. I had a gallon of Clorox bleach. How to prioritize what to take?

Take the toilet paper, leave the flour. Don't come back until it's safe.

It was a tense and harrowing thirteen-hour drive to Cincinnati that included a snowstorm in the mountains of Pennsylvania, one cat peeing in her box, one cat throwing up in her box, and the humans trying to use public bathrooms as infrequently as possible. We were getting phone calls and text messages about people in our shows who were getting sick. I checked our temperatures at every stop. Halfway through the drive Martha looked at me and said, "I think you should book that house for another two weeks." We rolled into Cincinnati at just after two in the morning. We immediately bubbled in with my brother and his family, and Charlotte joined us in Cincinnati not long after. We stayed for three months.

Miraculously, Martha and Tobi and I did not contract Covid-19 despite being surrounded by it. Both of our shows had numerous cases. Four of the six of us who performed on *Good Morning America* contracted Covid-19 and became symptomatic within days. Another show, *Moulin Rouge*, was severely affected. Many people in that company became ill, including the two lead male actors, one of whom became hospitalized in the ICU. A dresser at *The Phantom of the Opera* died. For weeks after Broadway shut down, it seemed that every time I opened my social media someone else in our community was ill or hospitalized.

We hunkered down in Cincinnati, and I could not imagine ever feeling safe enough to leave.

◆ ◆ ◆

Once we'd left New York it seemed all we did was watch the news about New York. New Yorkers were sick. Our many friends who'd stayed in New York were terrified, hearing sirens night and day. Tobi's friend Audrey and her brother Oliver did not leave their Midtown apartment for eighty-four days straight. People in our building were dying. One terrible night, a man leapt to his death off the roof of our building. Going back to New York was out of the question.

We followed Governor Cuomo's briefings like it was our job. The last thing Martha and I wanted, we agreed, was to be the New Yorkers who'd come to Cincinnati unknowingly sick and spread Covid-19. We did in Cincinnati what everyone around the world was doing: we stayed inside. My mind raced constantly. What if we got sick? What if we got *really* sick? I took everyone's temperature. I sprayed Clorox on everything. After I ran through the sickness fear, I jumped to financial fears. What if our work never came back? Did I have any other skills? Martha, who loves to drive, joked about getting her CDL (commercial driver's license) to become a cement truck driver. "I'll get my cup of coffee, load up the truck, and deliver cement. I'm totally into it!" I, on the other hand, had no plan. There were days when I, like the rest of the world, felt such despair at the rapid shutdown of the world and the loss of my job that if I made it through the day without taking a long nap, crying, or panicking every time anyone in my house sneezed, it was a massively good day. Many people took to social media, singing songs and trying to maintain a sense of normalcy. For a few weeks I posted cheery Instagram stories about staying strong and telling our audiences Broadway would be back. But I stopped when the Broadway League delayed the reopening *yet again* and I recorded a lengthy rant that turned into tears. Nobody needed me being a big bummer in their newsfeed and I was all out of funny stories.

Despite the lovely spring weather, the long walks, and making things as good as I possibly could, I was officially depressed. The *Come From Away* company leaned heavily on each other. We had Zoom catch-ups several times a week, all of us grateful to see each other and compare stories. Astrid, who'd been cast as Beulah, the character that told the joke from my very first audition, kept us all laughing on the calls. People were all over the country and in Canada. I can't really express to you how critical these Zoom hangouts were, for we'd been together for so long we could finish each other's sentences. There was a freedom to show up, however you were feeling that day, and know that even if all you could do was listen, that was enough.

We were all starving for information about when Broadway would come back. Even though announcements of each new date pushed the reopening further and further away, we kept telling our stupid stories and making each other laugh.

Meanwhile, I suddenly needed to transport my twelve-year-old and their golden retriever to their dad's in San Diego for the summer. Putting them on a plane seemed possible (planes were still flying) but not plausible. It was just too risky, and Tobi had already put their foot down. They would *not* get on an airplane.

So the question on the table in the spring of 2020 was how to safely get Tobi from one parent to the other with as minimal contact with the outside world as possible. We needed to socially distance from coast to coast. Driving our car meant constant exposure and risk by staying in hotels, eating out, and days of nothing but public bathrooms. Dirty gas station bathrooms make me nervous on a good day, let alone in a global viral outbreak.

I looked at Martha.

"What if. . ."

I stopped. I knew I had to be sure I was about to say something I meant, because I knew what her reply would be. Martha has a catch phrase, loved by both Tobi and Charlotte, who now enthusiastically scream it at the top of their lungs: "I'm totally into it!" I knew Martha would be totally into it. Was I? Uh, no. But I must tell you, this RV promise comes up a lot. Martha and Tobi have been looking at RVs for years. They have requirements. If a Pinterest board exists with a title like MAR AND TOBI'S DREAM RV, I would not be shocked. When a beautiful vacation spot shows up on TV, they nod quietly to each other like a secret handshake that says, "We'll go there in the RV." And I raise my eyebrows back at them to say, "You're always welcome to shower in my suite at the Westin."

I'd never seen myself in an RV. Or in an RV park. RVs are for Other People. Outdoor People. People who hunt and who were probably previously in the military.

But I had to admit, this plan was so good I was surprised Martha and Tobi hadn't hatched it themselves. I could get Tobi safely across the country by fulfilling my alleged promise to Martha. Two birds with one stone.

"Mar. What if we rent an RV and drive Tobi across the country?"

You can guess her response. If not, my kids will loudly reenact it for you.

CHAPTER 4

CRUISE AMERICA

On the advice of my uncle Bill, an RV lover, we found ourselves in Fairfield, Ohio, at an RV rental place called Cruise America. I'd called and spoken to George, the manager, days earlier, and he'd talked me through the ins and outs of renting an RV. My main takeaway from that phone call: it's shockingly similar to renting a car if your rental car had a toilet, a microwave, and a bed. You walk in, hand them your driver's license and a credit card, and you drive away. Main difference? The rental vehicle is the size of a London bus.

Martha and I had spent hours down the internet RV rabbit hole watching videos and learning about classes of RVs (we'll get to that in a minute), debating to buy or not to buy. I suppose it seems ludicrous to think we'd even entertain the idea of buying an RV because, well, we live on 43rd Street and 10th Avenue in Midtown Manhattan, which a vast majority of people might consider less than ideal for RV ownership. Undeterred, Martha and I really considered it, even as far as to research land in upstate New York where we could "buy to park" said purchased RV and visit it on our days off. Thank God one of us woke up after hours of online shopping to say, "WTF are we doing? We are unemployed."

George explained over the phone that Cruise America had great rental deals running, and a half-price-mile offer. Truth be told, without even haggling (and I love to haggle), the price was suddenly doable, though not exactly cheap. Cruise America primarily rents to European and Japanese tourists who flock to the National Parks in the Western US. Since international travel was basically shut down while the world waited out the virus, the company was eager for domestic travelers who might not care that they'd have to weave around various park closures and travel restrictions. Also in our favor was some world oil situation that was happening, causing gas prices to be as low as I'd seen in my adult life.

Martha and I had flirted with the idea of dropping Tobi and their dog Desi off in San Diego and then, with no jobs to return to for the foreseeable future, just staying out on the road until it was time to pick her up again. A total of ten weeks seemed financially impossible, but suddenly George was making it a real possibility. And we could do it in a rental.

Before we could commit (and by "we," I mean "me"), I wanted to take a look at the rig in person. I have no idea if people use the word "rig" when it comes to an RV, but I really like the sound of it. If I chewed tobacco, I would add a spit after saying it. "I better gas up my rig and pull out" (spit). During our phone conversation, George told me that the new sanitation rules prevented him from showing us anything in their stock. I figured I could take my woman and go check the outside of the rig (spit).

Fairfield, Ohio, is on the outskirts of Cincinnati and a place I knew by name only. I grew up and went to college in Cincinnati, but Fairfield, which is a combo platter of rural and industrial, had no purpose for me and my musical theater dreams. As we drove down Dixie Highway, Martha and I marveled at how long it would take to mow all of the fields and bonded over how we'd like to have that job.

The Cruise America RVs are recognizable from space as they have gigantic graphics all over them depicting various scenes of America, like Arches National Park, as well as a golden retriever whose little face peeks out through the door. "There!" Martha yelled, pointing to a small building in a sprawling parking lot full of various RVs, mostly privately owned but with some Cruise America RVs mixed in. We pulled in, and I immediately drove through the opening in the chain link fence to drive around the parking lot. A Cruise America RV emblazoned with a forest of Sonora cacti majestically lounged in front of the building, and someone, I had to assume George, was inside. I had not mentioned to George that we were coming, and my first instinct was to hide, which I suppose was just a sign of the times. Every TV commercial and billboard reminded us not to go out, to shelter in place, and yet here we were, unannounced in Fairfield. I quickly drove into the parking lot and pulled behind a Class A Motorhome, which is the biggest RV of all—think the size of a Greyhound bus—and a perfect shield between us and George.

We drove around and managed to find some Cruise America RVs in the back, and we compared sizes. We knew from the website that they came in a twenty-five-foot length and a thirty-foot length, and the question was: what's in five feet? We peered out through our car windows, but we couldn't see anything. Finally, more curious than nervous, we got out and looked in the windows of different RVs. We went in separate directions as we yelled to each other:

"This looks like the twenty-five."

"Honey, I think I found a thirty."

"Can you see the kitchen?"

After a minute a ruddy-faced fifty-something guy—George, I assumed—approached the fence. I shot a look toward Martha and said, "Be cool," like we were on a heist. But what I really meant was "stop holding my hand."

"Are you George?" I asked.

The chain link fence, like a prison fence, was tall and had barbed wire at the top. I wondered if snarling German shepherds protected these RVs and, with a chill up my spine and a glance behind me, I wondered on which side of the fence those beasts would appear.

"You're Sharon. I looked you up after we talked."

In our conversation I'd told George about coming from New York because of the Covid-19 outbreak, and what we do for a living. He asked the name of the show I was in and seemed impressed that we were on Broadway, but then also not that impressed because he'd never heard of the show itself. I get that. It was easier when I was in *Cats* or *The Phantom of the Opera*. Everyone knows those shows. My role is much bigger in *Come From Away*, and I am part of the original cast, so I am on the cast album, the theater equivalent of being a top pick in the NFL draft, but hey, George didn't know that, or care, and honestly, I didn't really care right at that moment either. I was in Fairfield, Ohio, in an RV parking lot, and I'd just stepped on a tiny fish, which made no sense at all.

"I told my wife about you, and we both looked at your picture. Seems like a nice thing, your show. Maybe we'll see it. I don't see many shows, but that one sounds good." George's sincerity stroked my ego. I felt "seen" as well as ashamed of myself.

Martha and I talked to George behind the prison fence for a long time. "You ladies sure will enjoy a cross-country trip. My wife and I just took one last year. I'm a proud right-wing Republican, but when I saw those National Parks, I decided if that's where my tax dollars are going, I'm okay with that."

My parents were Republicans, as were Martha's, so I'm comfortable with differing political viewpoints. However, being gay was relatively new to me, and more of a red alert when I meet someone who declares himself a staunch conservative. Immediate stomachache.

Meanwhile, Martha works with guys like George all the time and seemed completely unfazed. As a stage manager, she oversees managing the communication to the crews who provide props, sets, and lights. It's a small and familial world in the theater with tough IATSE (International Alliance of Theatrical Stage Employees) stagehands. Often, employees pass down their jobs from generation to generation. For example, my buddy Pete who does props on stage left at *Come From Away* has only two people who sub in for him if he needs a night off: his daughter Tess, and his niece Sarah. Martha loves guys like Pete and George, so she fell right into the role of "managing" and started asking George a million technical questions about whether we should get the twenty-five-footer or the thirty. At one point George was talking about traveling with his wife, and he asked, "Are you girls good friends? Me and my wife—this is my second wife—she and I spent so much time together on that trip that we realized we really do like each other. But if you aren't good friends, it's going to show up real fast."

Did he think we were friends or lovers? His comparison of his marriage to friends left me confused and worried. I grappled with why I cared, but I knew in my gut that George represented every person in my life that would be shocked that I'd married a woman, which included my dead parents. Thus, George's reaction became my mom and dad and every Republican's reaction (at least every Republican I'd ever known). I waited for the judgment and shock. The disdain.

Instead, George focused on the pros and cons of a twenty-five-footer vs. a thirty-footer. I focused on calming my pounding heart, ashamed to realize how nervous I was in this environment, so different from the safety of New York City, full of Pride flags celebrating out-ness. To be fair, the pride of out-ness makes me nervous, too. I glanced over at Martha, who seemed nonplussed. Actually, she seemed completely comfortable, her head thrown back and laughing about a joke I'd missed in my brain swirl of paranoia. Martha swears to this day he knew all along we were married. I'm still not so sure.

After a bit he decided he could show us the RV he was working on since he hadn't cleaned and sterilized it yet. We were desperate to see inside, so we agreed. As we walked over, I reminded her again, "Don't be affectionate." She nodded. I took that as an agreement. We stepped into the RV, and even I had to "oooh" and "ahhh." This really could be fun.

But Martha just couldn't stop calling me "honey."

"Honey! Sit in the driver's seat and look in the rear-view mirror. You can see the bed!" "Honey! I think the kitties would like to be right up here. It looks so cozy."

I tried to shush her. As I squeezed past her, out of earshot of George, I nudged her and whispered, "Stop calling me honey!" She either didn't hear me or she forgot. Or most likely? She didn't care. Moments later she was outside and yelling for "Honey!" to come see the storage capacity. Even with my unease that we would end up in a tragic homophobic nightmare, I had to laugh. There is no denying that Martha's ability to be completely comfortable in her skin is her most attractive quality.

I relaxed. George and I talked about high schools, and it turned out he was a year younger than me and went to Moeller, the "brother" all-boys' Catholic high school to my all-girls' Catholic high school, Ursuline Academy. We laughed that we were absolutely at the same dances and football games in high school, and somehow that gave me street cred with George. Soon enough his buddy Tony turned up, and he called him over. "Tony has to meet you. He goes to all the plays."

Tony was older than George and holding a hose. He owned all the property, including a bait shop, which explained the small dead fish I'd seen, and he was at work hosing out a truck. "Tony should be retired, but he still shows up and hoses out the trucks every day."

"Keeps my wife and me married," Tony laughed. Martha later told me she wanted to be Tony when she grows up. George wanted me to tell Tony the plot of the show I was in, just like I'd told him minutes before, so I repeated it all over again while Tony asked questions. Then Martha told them all about *Diana* and answered all the questions about what a stage manager does. It was fun, especially because in a world where Covid-19 lockdown kept most of us inside, we were outside, talking about future plans and making new friends.

By the end, Tony said he was coming with us, and George said he'd fix us up with a nice new RV for our trip. We all had a hard time saying goodbye. After so many weeks of quarantine, meeting new people felt like the sun coming out. "You girls sure are likeable. You're going to have a great time." As we drove out of the parking lot, I confessed to Martha how scared I'd been of George. She looked at me like I had three heads. "Just be yourself and don't worry about it. Those guys don't care." For the rest of the drive home, I basically hung my head in shame at how I'd so wrongly judged George based on his politics. Martha gave me a break. "You still worry what your parents would think about being married to me." She cracked a wide grin and bellowed loudly, "They'd love me!" I had to laugh because, of course, she was right.

George and Tony are now my friends on Facebook, and when I booked the rig (spit) weeks later, George told me to make sure his number was in my cell. "Text me anytime. You girls are my responsibility while you are out on the road."

Basically, we are now like siblings, after all.

And Martha really did call him with a million questions.

CHAPTER 5

ALL THINGS RV

There was a freedom in putting all our goods in a rolling home and taking our lives back. We'd been held hostage by this virus and now here we were, defying all odds, making our way. The gas was expensive—$88 the first time we filled up—but doable thanks to cheap gas prices nationwide. We'd all successfully used the toilet and overall it was no big deal. And by no big deal I mean it did not stink so badly that I gagged. I was anticipating a much-used church festival portapotty smell, but it was just a bathroom. Not to get bogged down in the bathroom, but since it was my number one concern and my number two concern (see what I did there?) I feel like dedicating a paragraph to the bathroom is worthwhile.

The fear? Seems gross. Reality? Isn't.

Had it been, I can promise you this fussy woman would have disembarked somewhere around Indianapolis and walked home. One quick side note if you are reading this book as an instruction manual for ALL THINGS RV (and why wouldn't you be?): I promise you that 100% of the time you will forget to put the hand soap away and 100% of the time you will hear a large "bang!" as if you'd run over a popcorn tin. That is the sound of your forgetfulness, the hand soap flying through the air. Remember to put the hand soap back, and by "back" I mean *in the sink*. Lots of stuff can go in the sink. For example, prior to pulling out every morning I put the fruit bowl in the kitchen sink. Worked like a charm. No more apples rolling all over the place.

Hold on a second! Since I have a trailer-park-filled brain about RVing, and as a total newbie, I am the perfect person to create a Newbie RV Primer. I will not be patronizing or mansplain. I give you my Girl Scout Honor. This is quite simply All You Need to Know.

Let's start with the basics. Types of RVs. Do not be intimidated, young Jedi. I did not know any of this prior to renting one. For the legal team, I do not verify the accuracy of this glossary.

RV

RV (Latin for Recreational Vehicle, *n*, noun) is a general term that encapsulates a lot of different vehicles, although the basic idea is the ability to drive and sleep in the same vehicle. Interchangeable in the layperson's vernacular: camper, mobile home, trailer, pop-up, fifth wheel, motorhome, camper van, and truck camper. This even includes brand-specific vehicles like Airstreams, Winnebagos, and VW Campers or VW Buses.

Used in a scene:

NEWBIE: "I'm thinking about renting an RV for the summer!"

RV DEALER: "I can get you set up. What kind are you looking at?"

NEWBIE: "There are kinds?"

RV DEALER (smugly to himself): *Newbie. They will wreck my rig for sure (spit).*

To the FTRV population[2] each vehicle is extremely, entirely, and totally different. In an attempt to catch up the general population with the FTRV crowd, I will clarify. I think (I hope) we *all* understand that a tiny home is different from an RV.

Distinction as a subset for your flashcard: Tiny Home (American for "Off the grid living in my parent's backyard," *f*, noun) is a permanent home that can be moved from place to place on wheels. Often seen in renovations and new builds on TV, where the people walk in and say, "Wow. It's so tiny!" A Tiny Home could be considered a trendier, more permanent cousin of the RV. From Martha: "They're more Millennial."

Distinction in a sentence:

"My ukulele and hemp milk fit snugly in my Tiny Home."

vs.

"My RV gets ten miles to the gallon."

Note: There are no RV renovation shows on HGTV.

MOBILE HOME VS. MOTORHOME

You think they are the same thing. Wrong. I thought so too, rookie. A mobile home—which is now more commonly called a manufactured home but also has gone by the less flattering slang of "trailer home"—prompting the loving and kind nickname "trailer trash" for its residents—is a prebuilt home that is taken somewhere on a truck bed and placed (usually) permanently. If you've watched *Ozark*

---

2   Full Time RVers are people who have sold their home and now live in an RV full-time. Like 365 days a year. Think *Nomadland*. This will be on the test.

on Netflix, this is where the Langmore family lives. No offense to the Langmores, but this is not the experience Martha and I were looking for.

A motorhome has a motor. You can drive it. It also has the defining feature of being an ALL-IN-ONE. You drive it, you cook in it, you sleep in it, you shower in it. It has a steering wheel *and* a toilet. So, as an example, if you are the passenger and you suddenly want a Diet Coke, you can just get up and walk to the fridge and get one. No need to stop driving. As of this writing, I really do not know about the legality of getting up without a seatbelt, but I'll get back to you if I get a ticket because I had an intense craving for hummus and carrots while barreling across Indiana. The point is, it does not get pulled by something. It drives itself. Motorhomes can be used for other non-traveling purposes, like a blood drive or even as a school guidance counselor's office. I spent a great deal of my high school years sitting in a motorhome in the parking lot of my all-girls Catholic high school talking about all of the reasons I could not manage to finish my Latin homework. It seemed perfectly normal at the time, to hike through the slushy parking lot in freezing cold temperatures in my clogs and uniform skirt, but now I see how odd it was. I do remember there was a bathroom in there that I was not allowed to use, and I also remember that I insisted on sitting in the driver's seat while we talked.

I'm sorry, reader. I don't mean to make things more difficult now, just as you are really feeling "RV-ducated," but I must add to the curriculum. There are certain classes of motorhomes.[3] Let's talk singers, for example. You'd never call a soprano an alto, right? Or

---

3   Note: This really is something you need to know, so get your highlighters ready. A wrong answer leads you to myriad problems.

confuse a ballet dancer with a tango dancer? Or just say all pasta is spaghetti? Sacrilege.

TYPES OF MOTORHOMES

Class A

This is the mothership of all motorhomes. It looks like a bus. It's gigantic, swanky, and expensive. A Class A motorhome usually has all the bells and whistles, like a washer and dryer (I am not kidding) and a host of other perks.[4] If you are looking for a way to transport your rock and roll band while on tour, you are going to customize the crap out of a Class A motorhome, but regular families also own Class A motorhomes, including my uncle Bill, the only RV owner I know, who became a go-to for all of our early planning. He steered us toward buying an RV thinking we could probably sell it at the end of the summer and earn all our money back. Given the state of our work (none) and my bank account at the time (dwindling) I did not consider it, but he was right. I could have sold that thing for a pretty penny. He steered us away from a Class A, telling us this luxury rig can be a target for break-ins. He tows his jeep behind his, making it, in total, about 52 feet long. For perspective, dear reader, a Toyota Corolla is 15 feet long. A full-size school bus is 35 feet long. The White House is 70 feet long. So, my uncle Bill drives something that is roughly longer than a school bus, but shorter than the White House.

---

4   Perks include but are not limited to: heated floors, leather reclining sectional couch, exterior entertainment system with 50" LED TV, satellite dish, dishwasher, garbage disposal, two bathrooms, his and her sinks, bathtub, central vacuum system, king-size bed, a fireplace, a walk-in closet, and our personal favorite (and most frequently seen): a telescoping flagpole complete with spotlights to illuminate the American flag.

Class B

This motorhome is more like a tricked-out van.[5] Think VW Camper or Mercedes Sprinter, both super cute by the way, but small. I remember when I was in drama school, my acting teacher told my class, "A real actress lives out of her van and only needs her cat and *Time* magazine."

I'm pretty sure she was talking about a Class B motorhome, but after my 32 years as a professional actress, I can confidently tell you I didn't understand anything else she was saying. Also, how would someone have a cat in a van? And how is your *Time* magazine delivered? It stuck with us, though, and when my best friend Maryday quit her acting career she cried to me, "I want a couch! I want a couch!"

See, now, if she'd had a Class A motorhome, she could have had a couch AND an acting career. Also, she eventually married my brother, which is just a bonus and could be extra credit on the test, so keep it in mind.

Class C

I'm going to call this the Goldilocks of a motorhome because it's not too big and it's not too small. If Martha were here, she would want me to tell you it's built on a truck chassis, but I don't really know what that means. What I *do* know is I've driven a U-Haul truck, and this looks like it's about the size of a moderate U-Haul, so I could imagine driving it. The size is somewhere between "not bad" and "terrifying" to drive, so that seems like the right thing. The Class C usually takes "regular" gas (cheaper and easier to find) and comes in a variety of lengths. If Tobi were here, they'd want

---

5   For a more in-depth study of Class Bs, explore Frances McDormand's van in *Nomadland*. Dioramas of that van can be submitted for extra credit.

me to tell you it has one of those beds that sits over the cab of the truck which, when you are twelve, is essential. Class C met all of our needs.

Beyond the motorhome/mobile home is another whole class of RVs that you *pull* behind a truck or a big SUV. These are aptly called trailers. Again, there are several types and then variations within those types, but I will give you the down and dirty basics.

PULLING IT: THE DOWN AND DIRTY BASICS

Travel Trailers

Like motorhomes without the motor, a travel trailer hitches on the rear of your vehicle, and you essentially pull it. If you've seen Lucy and Desi in the 1954 classic *The Long, Long Trailer* you've got a good idea what I am talking about. These are (generally speaking) less expensive than a motorhome and have the bonus of separating from the truck/SUV you are using to pull it. Why does that matter? I guess because if you get to a campground and you "hook up" to water and electric and sewer, but then you realize you are out of tampons, you can just unhook the car and drive to the CVS but leave the trailer intact. If our car, a Honda CRV, had enough power to pull a trailer, we probably would have gone for a trailer, but the CRV can basically pull a toaster oven and that's it. Showbiz note: Trailers are also used on film and TV sets for dressing rooms and hair and makeup. The bigger the star, the nicer the trailer. I have had a trailer on a movie set, but don't be intimidated by my fanciness because the movie I shot was so bad it was never released. I'm not saying it was released to bad reviews. I am saying it was *so bad* it was never released. Side note: Martha's grandparents took her and her brother James on weekend excursions in their trailer. Many of the *Martha Donaldson Dreams of Retirement in an RV* are born from these memories.

Fifth Wheel Trailers (also called Fivers)

Does a fifth wheel trailer have a fifth wheel? No. It's a travel trailer that is easier to drive because of some fancy U-shaped hitch invented back in the horse and buggy days. You think I'm making that up. I'm totally not. Google it. Apparently, it's better? And easier? I think it has to do with physics or something, I read about it and promptly realized I was thinking about making a turkey sandwich for lunch so I can't explain it. Basically, the deal is that you hook it into a big clamp thingamabob in the bed of your pickup truck, and then magically you can turn the whole thing more safely. Fifth wheels are enormously popular.

Pop-ups

These trailers are smaller than regular trailers because they have a pop-up capacity. If you ever watched the Oprah and Gayle series where they do an overnight in Yosemite, you know they had a pop-up trailer. It's somewhere between a trailer and a giant tent. It involves a fairly elaborate setup.

So that's it! There are other kinds of trailers, and God knows people do all kinds of car camping and variations on all these themes, but these are the basics.

PARK AND SLEEP

Now that you have the RV of your dreams, where can you stay in this beauty? Oh sure, we all know there are some elaborate campgrounds, many with swimming pools and restaurants. But what if you want to save some cash? Can you just pull over and sleep anywhere?

Sleeping over in your RV isn't as random and easy as it seems. You can usually stop at a rest stop or a truck stop and park and sleep for free, but there are things to know before you go.

Important: Make sure you know the total length of your rig. This will be the very first question and is crucial to booking you in the correct spot. Nothing will piss off a camp host faster than if you book a spot meant for a Fiat (car analogy) and you show up in a Cadillac El Dorado. Size matters.

Decision time. You will need to decide if you want to hook up. Hooking up is more than a college challenge on a Friday night. In RV talk it has to do with electric and water and being able to dump your tanks. At the more commercial campgrounds you often get some shaky Wi-Fi and even can hook up to their cable TV system. It's very rare to find a hookup in a state or national park, but in places like Yellowstone there are dump stations and places to fill your water tanks near the campground entrances. Forget about Wi-Fi. Forget about cell service. It's shocking and somewhat awesome to discover that people all over America choose to go off the grid. Over time you'll discover what the perfect balance is for you. I realized if I had to choose between electric or cell service, I would choose cell service every time. That's how addicted I am to texting. I know. It's a problem.

Here are some terms and ideas you never thought you'd need to know, and probably still don't, but I am going to teach you because I had to learn them, so you do, too.

KOA (Kampgrounds of America)

KOA is a network of privately owned campgrounds all around the country. You join the KOA community, plug in the dates you want, and book a certain kind of site, depending on the size and type of your rig. This was described to us by Uncle Bill as the "Holiday Inn" of campgrounds. You pull in, you check in, they give you a map to your site, you hook up, and you light your fire for s'mores. If you don't have wood, don't worry! You can buy wood and all of your s'more-making treats right there in the KOA camp store. Bada Bing! Bada Boom! We stayed at a lot of KOAs in our time, especially when we were with the kids. They are crowded and not very pretty, but the people are friendly, and the sites absolutely get the job done.

State Parks and National Parks

RVing in a state or national park is really the way to go. The sites are much more primitive than a KOA or privately owned campsite, but they are also cheaper and much more beautiful. These are the campsites you see on commercials. They often sell out quickly. They usually have a fire ring and sometimes a grill, and that's it. Expect to have no hookups at all (boondocking, see below), which is much better for stargazing and a traditional camp experience. The parks vary greatly, so read the online reviews and if people keep talking about certain site numbers, pay attention and try to book those sites. They are usually level and have better views. And if the site comes equipped with a bear box,[6] use it.

Boondocking (also called drydocking)

This is parking your RV without hooking it up. RVs can live off the grid for a period of time, depending on how big your water and

---

6   A bear box is a metal box that is bear proof. Campsites in bear country will demand that you put all food items either back in your camper or in the provided bear box. This includes (but is not limited to) all food, candles, toothpaste, and anything with a scent. We almost got a ticket in Yellowstone for leaving something out, so pay attention to the rules. Unless you really want to see a bear. And by "see a bear" I mean "get the shit scared out of you by a bear in your campsite."

septic tanks are, and how much juice you have in your generator, should you need to use it. However, nearly all campgrounds limit the time you can use a generator because they are L-O-U-D and considered bad manners.

Wallydocking

Boondocking in a Walmart parking lot. I guess a lot of people knew that was possible, but I sure didn't! Other major chains allow boondocking, including Cracker Barrel and some Home Depots, but you have to get permission from a manager.

Moochdocking

My favorite of the "docking" terms, this is when you stay in a friend's driveway and run an extension cord into their house and use their water via hose, thereby "mooching" off of their paid resources. When I was a kid, my dad's childhood friend drove his family up from Houston in an RV and moochdocked off of us for what seemed like forever. I was young and all I remember is a long, orange all-weather extension cord that ran out the door and a ton of kids all over our house. I think they had seven kids, and I think the bathroom was occupied 24/7. We all breathed a sigh of relief when they left, mostly because my mom just about pulled her hair out trying to keep the house in order and everyone fed. As an adult I wonder what that electric bill was like. I told my sister we were visiting friends of ours in Sonoma, California, and were considering asking them if we could run power from their house. Her answer was dark. "That's a really shady thing to do."

Harvest Host

This is a relatively new way to boondock we found through a hefty Instagram ad campaign. For about $60 a year, you can join a Harvest

Host community where farmers, wineries, small businesses, muse-ums, and even some golf courses allow you to boondock overnight. In return you are expected to buy some of their eggs or a bottle of wine or support them in some way. The locations are all over the country and are (mostly) beautiful. Despite looking at them all over the place, in truth we only spent one night at a Harvest Host, in the parking lot of a brewery in Montana. We bought beer and we were put off by other RVs who had barking and lunging dogs. With no camp host to monitor the grounds, it felt a little dicey.

WATER COLORS

As you can imagine, an RV can only boondock for a certain length of time before the tanks need to be filled or emptied. Since we used our RV bathroom exclusively and our kitchen for nearly every meal, the proper filling and emptying of our tanks was paramount. Being a stage manager, Martha volunteered to be the tank manager, while I managed all interior tidying and decor. But I ended up taking over tank duties (foreshadowing! highlight this!) so I will lay out the tank basics.[7]

Black Water

This is the sewage tank. It must be dumped in a "dumping station" or hooked up to the sewage line in a campground. My English teacher from high school came over for a porch visit before we left, and her parting words were "Don't forget to clean out the shitter." She has such a way with words.

---

7   Suggested footwear is a closed toe with the ability to hose those shoes off immediately as accidents happen and it is completely, totally, horrifically disgusting. So. Gross. I can't stop picturing it. OMG.

Gray Water

This is the dirty water from the kitchen and bathroom sink as well as the shower. This fills up quickly, and (we discovered) can be used as a thank-you gift when leaving an arid climate. We filled ten-gallon buckets and dumped the (still fairly gross) gray water on our friend's trees that were suffering from the severe California drought.

Fresh Water

Holds all the fresh water for all your freshwater needs. I think you can usually drink it. If I end up with a parasite, please tell the EPA to test the freshwater tank. Thanks.

Stinky Slinky

This is a hose that collapses together and spreads apart like a slinky. It is used to empty the black water tank. There is a specific way to dump the tanks. Dump the black water, then the gray. Why? The gray water washes away any residual, um, remnants from the black water. Think: The gray water is like the toilet bowl brush for the hose.

Look. I have to stop here. I could have a glossary the length of a Class A pulling a Jeep, but we really have to get on with the story. I will explain more as we go. If you have a question, please submit it to the "Huh?? What??" box.

Now, before we actually pull out in the behemoth, I have a quick story about what happened to me in another crisis, and what happened when I called home.

CHAPTER 6

THE POOLMASTER'S DAUGHTER

I felt it.

I woke up as I was thrown to the floor by the initial slam, landing on my side near the floor-to-ceiling plate glass window, narrowly missing a glass side table. Not thinking, not knowing what to do, I crawled around my high-rise hotel room in Pasadena for the duration of the earthquake as the shaking took over. I later found out the 1994 Northridge earthquake was considered short, only twenty seconds long, but I can tell you from firsthand experience, as you crawl around a moving floor while hearing glass shatter all around you, that twenty seconds feels like the end of your life.

When the shaking stopped, I reached for the remote and turned on the TV, surprised the power was still on. I was in shock, but I also wondered if I was being a baby about it. People who live in California tend to roll their eyes about earthquakes and ride them out like a badge of honor, akin to the way New Yorkers smugly stand on a shaking subway without holding on, giving the tourists around them long looks and irritated sighs as they fall all over the train with each lurch of the car. I figured if the news was covering the earthquake (or maybe it was a bomb? a gas explosion?) I could gauge my reaction. The local NBC overnight news came on, with two nervous-looking anchors seated at a desk, trying to calmly break the news.

"At 4:30:55 am, just seconds ago, a massive earthquake rocked the greater Los Angeles area. At this point we know very little, but we are anticipating severe injuries and casualties."

Immediately the room started shaking again with a severe aftershock. Both news anchors threw themselves under the desk as the female anchor screamed, "IF ANYONE CAN HEAR US, THE LOS ANGELES AREA IS EXPERIENCING A MAJOR EARTHQUAKE AND WE ARE IN THE NEWSROOM . . . HERE IT GOES AGAIN . . . OH MY GOD!!!!"

I turned it off immediately. I had no time for unhelpful hysterics. The room was still.

I got up from my hands and knees and wildly looked around the hotel room. *What do you do in an earthquake?*

I am from the Midwest; I know to go to the basement during a tornado and I know how to drive in a blinding snowstorm, but I am woefully undereducated in the finer points of earthquake survival. I raced through my disaster awareness protocol. Stop, drop, and roll if you are on fire. Get to high ground in a flood. Carry an umbrella in flying cicada season. Earthquake? I was blank. I carefully looked out the window—mine was thankfully intact—and saw only shattered glass on the ground. I went to the door and opened it, looking down the long hallway of identical doors. Nobody. Should I leave? Should I take the elevator? Leaving and getting to solid ground seemed smart. An elevator seemed risky. Instructions on the inside of my hotel room door caught my eye. Bingo! Surely a hotel in Southern California would have what-to-do-in-case-of-earthquake instructions. Every restaurant around the world had instructions on how to give someone the Heimlich in case of choking. Subway trains had pull-here-in-case-of-emergency levers. I closed the door and wildly scanned the various notices the Hyatt Corporation felt I needed to know in case of emergency:

Rack Rate

In Case of Fire

Put Valuables in Your Room Safe

How to Lock Your Door

I ran around and opened every drawer. I found a Bible, which I tossed on the bed, suddenly acutely aware that my fallen-Catholic relationship with God might need immediate reconsidering. I found a pen and Hyatt stationery, which I also kept out in case I needed to write my final thoughts as I died in whatever horrible way people die in earthquakes.

Otherwise? Nothing. Not one scrap of instruction for what to do in an earthquake.

I called the front desk. A high, shaky female voice, attempting to sound calm, answered with her standard greeting:

"Good morning. Welcome to the Pasadena Hyatt. This is Lindsey. How may I direct your call?"

I was so relieved to talk to Lindsey, who was going to make everything better and also save my life. To be honest, a slightly sturdier name like Martha or Carol might have made me feel better, but I was stuck with Lindsey.

"Lindsey! My name is Sharon Wheatley. I am on the 14th floor, and I don't know what to do. That was an earthquake, right? What am I supposed to do?"

Silence.

I waited.

"Lindsey? Are you there?"

"Yes, ma'am."

"Do you have any instructions for me?"

"I'm sorry, ma'am. I am not allowed to give out any instructions at this time."

What?? Did I hear that right?

So, I said, "What?? Did I hear that right?"

Lindsey stuck to her script. "I am not allowed to give out any instructions at this time."

The room started shaking again, softer this time, but still horrifying, with a small aftershock.

"Lindsey, did you feel that? Did you *feel* that?"

Lindsey was shaken, literally. "Yes, ma'am, I did."

"Okay, Lindsey, listen. I need you to tell me something. I have no idea what to do. Do I go outside? Do I stay here?"

"Ma'am, I have no instructions for you."

And while maybe some of the details of this story are slightly fuzzy or could be contested in a court of law, the memory of what I said back to shaky Lindsey of the Pasadena Hyatt front desk is as clear as day.

I crazily yelled, "LINDSEY. I AM FROM OHIO. YOU HAVE TO TELL ME WHAT TO DO."

Lindsey hung up, which seemed fair.

I started to make another call, to my parents, desperate to talk to them, even more desperate to be with them, to be safely five years old again and in their earthquake-proof house. My dad, specifically, has an answer for every situation. In massive thunderstorms we would sit and count between lightning bolt and thunderclap to gauge the distance. When the strike and the boom were one second apart my dad would move us to the basement. "Okay, kid, it's getting close. Let's move out." And we'd head to the basement and play pool until the sky was quiet again. Basically, I needed my dad to tell me the "playing pool" equivalent for an earthquake. Where do I go to be safe? As I dialed him, the room started shaking again. I slammed the phone back down and rode it out.

One thing was crystal clear. No more phone calls. I had to get out.

I heard voices in the hallway and ran to the door, pulling it open like my life depended on it, which it did.

I saw my friends and castmates Traci Lyn and Eileen in the hall. We were all in Pasadena doing a national tour of *Les Misérables*, traveling around the country. Eileen and Traci Lyn were sharing a hotel room, trying to save some of their per diem. So smart. Why wasn't I frugal enough to have a roommate? Jealous of their shared terror, I glommed on to them for dear life.

"Hey, you guys. Hey, hi. Where are you going? What are we supposed to do? I'm going with you."

I shut my door and joined them without waiting for any response. We were all in our pajamas, in our twenties, and terrified. Eileen was from New York and hysterical (not helpful), but Traci Lyn was from Texas and had that kind of cowgirl *we can handle this* spirit, so she was immediately our leader.

Traci Lyn decided we should take the stairs and go outside. Eileen and I agreed, not because we thought it was a good idea, but because we were following Traci Lyn, who was our hero, our leader, the chosen one, the earthquake master. "Besides," Traci Lyn pointed out, "maybe they'll have coffee."

Such a sensible and non-panicked idea.

We pulled open the door to the stairwell and looked up and down. We heard voices. Traci Lyn recognized the voices and said, "It's Steve.

This is what we should do." Steve was on the crew and in charge of keeping us safe on stage, so now we were going to follow Steve.

◆ ◆ ◆

We made our way down the fourteen stories and into the lobby, startled by the bright lights and piped-in music. The furniture was all over the place, moved around by the earthquake, but we made our way to the front doors, which miraculously still slid open automatically. I was reminded of disaster movies where the slightest bits of retained normalcy seem shocking.

Most of our cast and crew were out on the sidewalk in front of the hotel, talking and comparing stories. I looked up and saw the floor above mine had lost its windows. Our stage manager, Mike, did a quick head count, and we were all accounted for except for two people who were a newly formed couple now sharing a room. They did eventually turn up and won the story of the night. They'd been having sex in front of the sliding mirrored closet doors when the quake struck, and the doors had fallen on them. They were fine and laughing, telling everyone every detail. I noted that things could still be funny in an emergency, and I tried to laugh. But I couldn't.

Despite being out of the building, I was still very scared. I stood near Mike, finding his presence both soothing and functional. He was my boss, but, more importantly, all critical information would come to him first. By standing right next to him, I could eavesdrop and immediately hear things I was supposed to hear later.

I overheard a whispered conversation about whether we'd be performing that night and while I could not hear *exactly* what was being said because the actors were still laughing about the sexcapades, I for sure heard Mike say something like "Well, you know, the show must go on."

Does the show have to go on after a massive earthquake? And if it does, do *I* have to go on? All I wanted to do was make a break for it to a land that stood still. I wondered if the airports were open. I wondered if it was safer to drive. I wondered if there would be an aftershock or, worse, the *big* one, and the earth would open up and swallow us all alive. I didn't feel safe anywhere, but I certainly would not feel safe climbing around on the massive two-story set of *Les Miserables*, the show we were allegedly doing that night because some jerk in the year 19-whatever said the show must go on. I decided Mike was not to be trusted, but he might have one piece of important information.

"Hey, Mike, any idea where there might be a pay phone?"

I had to talk to my parents. My mom and dad were on Eastern time. I checked the time; it was 4:45 am in LA, making it 7:45 am in Cincinnati. I could see the lobby TVs playing through the windows— *BREAKING NEWS: MAJOR EARTHQUAKE IN LOS ANGELES AREA*—with live footage of collapsed buildings and raging fires. My parents, avid TV watchers, were probably completely freaked out; they probably thought I was dead, or, worse, pinned alive.

Mike pointed me towards a long line in the lobby where other hotel guests had already started making calls.

I raced to the long phone line. My mom left for work in fifteen minutes, and I wondered if she would go. Was she sitting in front of the TV, ringing her hands in the way she habitually did, worrying about me the way she'd worried about my brother years ago when he'd attended the infamous Who concert where kids were crushed to death racing for seats? When he'd finally walked through the door hours later, stoned and unaware that anything had happened, my mother collapsed to the floor sobbing with relief. I wanted to facilitate my mother collapsing on the floor with relief. Her relief meant I was okay. She was a great barometer for worry.

As independent and worldly as I was, making more money than my mom and dad combined, traveling the country, "adulting," as my daughter now calls it, I missed my mother so ferociously in that moment it almost knocked the wind out of me. I could imagine her buzzing around the house, getting ready for work. She was a classic morning person, who thrived with the routine of a 9-5 job. She dressed up and wore heels and took her lunch in a Russian dolls set of Tupperware, including a big container of lettuce and tuna or deli meat, as well as an extra smaller Tupperware inside it, housing her low-calorie vinaigrette salad dressing. Snapped into the lid were her folding utensils. Mom ate at her desk while simultaneously working and cracking jokes with the UPS guys. She then used her lunch break to take a power walk "in the sunshine." My mother loved to work. She loved the schedule of it, she loved the routine of it, she loved getting up and looking nice for it, and, most of all, she loved getting away from my dad for the day. If I could not reach her, I could always reach him. He was always home. If my mother was a barometer for worry, my father was the guy who would tell me what to do in a crisis.

In sharp contrast to my busy mom, my dad loved not working. He regularly declared, "No one is going to put me in a cubicle and tell me what to do!" Statements like this caused my mother to arch her eyebrow and remind him her job paid for his precious cable news. He'd roar with laughter and say, "OK, honey, OK. You can pay the little bills. But I bring in the big bucks." My mom would inevitably do something like pull the plug from the TV and walk out, and he would laugh and call her a "dickens." I would plug the TV back in, both entertained and nervous. My parents were funny, but not for the faint of heart.

My dad was an entrepreneur and a salesman. He'd sold a plethora of things in his life—cars, bras, insurance policies—but his big money maker was his swimming pool company, PoolMaster of Cincinnati, which he owned and operated for my entire childhood. It had closed after he'd run out of business by basically building pools for every rich person in Cincinnati from 1970 to 1990. By 1994, he'd created a job working occasional job fairs. He was able to work when he felt like it, and he was his own boss, so he stayed up late and slept in until noon. My dad, although he never studied or worked in science, had an exceptional aptitude for it.

One hundred percent of the time, if you called my parents' house before 12 pm, you were waking my father up. That never stopped him from answering the phone, though, which was perched right next to his head by the bed. He would pick it up on the first or second ring without opening his eyes, drop the receiver, and curse, like a drunk answering the phone after a three-day bender.

It was my turn to call. I dialed in my calling card number and their phone number and waited while it rang. I noticed the hotel had rolled out a free breakfast and the phone line disappeared. Pastries and coffee became more important than communicating, at least for a minute.

My dad picked up the receiver and immediately dropped it. I heard, distantly, "Oh hell, hold on a minute."

There were sounds of banging as the receiver was dragged up from the floor by the cord and copious amounts of throat clearing before a sleepy, yet passable, "Well, hello there."

My father always answered the phone as if he knew who was calling, and what's more, that he knew you'd be calling at just that moment.

"Dad! It's okay. I'm fine." I was so relieved to hear his voice. I knew they must be so worried about me, especially now that I knew from some of the native Californians in the cast that this was a REAL earthquake, and a BIGGIE, not just some earth-moving Carole King song lyric type of event. This was, like, a natural disaster, like a RED CROSS IS COMING kind of disaster. Doing exactly what one might expect of the youngest child who is also an actress, I started to cry, some might say on cue.

"Hiya, kid!" He seemed unfazed. This was unfair. It was my big moment. I kept going.

"I'm calling to say I'm okay. I'm not hurt," I sobbed.

"Are you crying?"

I'm pretty sure he sat up. Now we were getting somewhere.

"What time is it, anyway?"

"Look at the news."

"The news? Hold on. Let me get the remote. I turned it down a little while ago. Looks like something is burning."

I could hear Katie Couric's voice getting louder. *Reports are coming in from Los Angeles, where this densely populated area was just struck by a major . . .*

Once my dad could focus on the TV he said, "It looks like LA had a whopper of an earthquake!"

"Dad. I'm *in* Los Angeles. Remember? I'm here."

"Wait a minute. What? Oh, that's *right*! You told me last night. You're telling me you're in LA right now?"

"Yes!" I started to cry again.

His voice became low and serious.

"Did you feel it?"

"Yes! It knocked me out of bed! But I'm okay!" I cried harder.

He gasped for breath.

"Hot damn, kid! You just went through a 6.7 magnitude earthquake? I have *always* wanted to be in an earthquake! Now *this* is a great adventure! Tell me everything!"

This was not the response I'd anticipated. I expected things more in line with what other parents said to their kids, like "Thank God you're okay!" or "Don't take the elevator!" or "Stand in a doorway!" Later, when I reached my mom, her reaction was pragmatic and parental. "We have friends, the Browns, who live in Pasadena. Betsy is coming to pick you up, and you can stay at their house until you leave the LA area. I want you out of that high-rise."

But in the early morning hours of January 17th, I stood in the lobby of the Hyatt and talked my dad through every detail of my traumatic experience/adventure. He laughed heartily about the news anchors diving under the desk. "Sounds smart, though. That's a lot of weight hanging above them with all the studio lights." He thought I should find Lindsey at the front desk and introduce myself, insisting that I might be the person to help put together a safety plan for earthquakes for the Hyatt chain. "I was a Safety Engineer in the Navy. I can help you with that. We can call it *Escape the Quake*." The PoolMaster loved to name things.

An avid science buff, my dad barraged me with science facts saved up for just this moment. In soothing and sometimes mind-numbing detail, he taught me all about the science of earthquakes and why they can't be predicted. He talked about the Japanese engineers who studied swaying bamboo in earthquakes and went on to build high-rises on rollers to withstand the shake. "Did you hear a loud sound?" he asked. "I did," I told him. "That was probably the building rolling!" He was right. Known as the Northridge earthquake, it was the largest earthquake in the US in years. Most importantly, and this was the rolling sound, it caused my hotel to do something it was built to do: literally roll.

His excitement about the geology and engineering weren't particularly interesting to me, but his enthusiasm and desire to share the experience with me made everything not just bearable, but more fun. Later, he'd answer the phone saying, "How big was it? Did it shake you good?" knowing I'd only called in the middle of the night because there was an aftershock.

The show performed the night of the earthquake despite a curfew in LA. Being in Pasadena, we were in a different county, so we went on as planned. As I walked in the stage door, I passed by dumpsters full of sheetrock that had fallen from the ceiling, which was more than slightly unnerving. We had a pre-show safety meeting where Mike told us to "do what we felt comfortable doing." Considering *Les Miserables* had a tall, moving barricade as the major set piece, from which we often dangled many stories up, sometimes even upside down, the moment-to-moment decision about what felt safe kept us all on pins and needles. We had only one minor aftershock during the show, but it was enough to make us wonder what the hell we were doing on that stage. Personally, I tried to find my way under any set piece that resembled a doorway or a solid table, and I sang from under there. It was kind of like Chicken Little does *Les Miserables*.

Dad woke me up the next morning, calling me at the Browns' house to excitedly say, "Hey, hey, hey! You've really made it now, kid. You guys are in *USA Today*! You'll remember this for the rest of your life! It's in black and white!" Sure enough, there was an article covering the decision that *The Show Must Go On!* despite the dangerous working conditions for the cast and crew. My dad cut it out and it lived, taped, to his end table for a couple of years, next to his water glass and TV remotes.

When I saw the wrinkled paper many months later, I noticed a little note in the margin: "She's on a great adventure!"

I couldn't help but think of him, constantly, as I drove around the country during this crazy time. He would have laughed and had an opinion on everything. But mostly he would have told me to focus on enjoying it. "This is a great adventure, kid. Don't be scared, just drive," he would have said. "Show your kids how to have fun."

I have to agree with him.

After all, I am the PoolMaster's daughter.

CHAPTER 7

THE GOLF BALL

"Now?" I yelled back. I heard the golf ball rolling and then a distinct *plunk plunk plunk* as it dropped down the stairs.

"Nope," Tobi said, too quietly.

"Honey, can you be a little louder? It's hard to hear you up here." I worked hard to keep the edge out of my voice. I am forever working to keep the edge out of my voice.

"Mom," Tobi said. "Listen. I'm hungry and I don't really know what I'm doing and *Desi!*" I turned around in the seat to look back just in time to see Desi, the insatiable golden retriever, steal Tobi's cookie off the dinette, leaving a slobbery trail of crumbs.

I swallowed my frustration—we all know not to leave food anywhere within Desi's reach. For all of Desi's laid-back fluffy vibe, there's a skilled thief just under the surface. I reminded myself, *they're doing the best they can.* I reminded myself, *we are all doing the best we can. And Tobi is only twelve.*

"Tobs, you're doing great. Hang in there. Find the golf ball. Here." I handed them a brand-new headlamp. "Martha got us all headlamps." They put it on and were delighted to find myriad bulb settings, which they ran through in a dizzying light show. "Can you please make it steady? The strobe thing is going to give me a seizure."

I rolled down the window and tried to find Martha in the rear-view mirror. If I hit the brakes she showed up in the red glow of the light. Since our rental RV had no rear window, I had to rely on the side-view mirrors, which were currently set for Martha. I was a 5'4" driver in a seat designed for a 5'8" driver, driving the last leg of a twelve-hour trek that was supposed to be a six-hour trek.

◆ ◆ ◆

"Martha, honey?" If I added "honey" I sounded nicer. "We're rolling to the right."

"Yup. Hold on a second."

I heard her trying the back storage doors. Suddenly, she was at my window. "I need the keys."

I turned off the RV and handed her the keys.

"I put the levelers on the—"

"Left side," she said "I know. I moved them."

"Why?" I yelled too loudly into the darkness. Her need to rear-range made me bananas. "I had it all organized."

She reappeared at the window. "I put all the tools and stuff on the right."

Oh my God, I thought, please just hurry up and get the thing leveled already so we can build a fire and eat hot dogs to make this child happy.

In my outside voice I said, "Great." It was not a nice great.

She disappeared back into the darkness, and I heard things being moved around. While I was sitting in the dark, I assessed the KOA campground. I'd picked the "Historic Route 66 KOA in St. Louis, MO" as our first stop because it was exactly six hours from Cincinnati, where we'd started this trip twelve hours earlier, doubling the GPS calculation. According to the reviews, this KOA was traditionally sold out due to its proximity to the nearby giant theme park, Six Flags. Because of Covid-19, Six Flags was closed, as was everything. I noticed the pool and outdoor picnic area had caution tape and handwritten "Closed" signs. In June 2020, even the outdoors was closed.

St. Louis was stop #1 of six stops that would get us across the country, and our first day had been a busy one. My older child, Charlotte, had graduated from college, in a pandemic-inspired ceremony, over Zoom earlier in the day. The pomp and circumstance involved her and her roommates, drunk, knighting each other as their names were called. Charlotte said no one had worn pants and "it was perfect." I had the mixed feeling of relief that she'd made it fun and sorrow over missing the formality of a large university graduation. Instead of the previous plan of taking the weekend off of my job, flying to Chicago, renting an Airbnb and navigating a tricky weekend with her dad, his new wife, me, and my wife, I'd instead tuned in from our RV somewhere in Indiana, which, given the year we'd had so far, seemed anticlimactic, yet perfectly normal.

Martha reappeared at the window.

"I think your golf ball idea is a genius one. Let's give it a go."

We'd already *given it a go* and the golf ball had plunked down the stairs, but I did not say that out loud either because, seriously, right this moment I was the crabbiest person alive.

Martha continued, "I am going to try stacking three levelers on the left side. You think? On both of the wheels?"

I corrected her. "It rolled right. So, it's pitching down and slightly back on the right."

"Aha. OK. I'll try two on the back tire. Hold on a second."

Tobi was quietly sitting in the red glow of their headlamp in the back.

"Kid. How're you doing?"

"I'm hungry."

"Me too."

"Is every day going to be this long?"

"I hope not. It's just the first day and we drove slowly and stopped a lot. But it's kinda cool, right?"

"Can I ride up in my bed tomorrow?"

Tobi was sleeping in the bed above the cab, and I worried about slamming on the brakes and them flying back 30 feet. I also knew the dogs would circle and bark if Tobi got up there, because they felt it was their constitutional right to do all things always.

"I don't think it's safe to ride up there. Hey, I have an idea. Do you want to leash up the dogs and go look around?"

I wondered if I was right to send them out alone. My snobbery kicked in. What were we doing here? Who sleeps in an RV park? Are there kidnappers lurking behind the bushes? I sounded like a helicopter parent. I was being ridiculous.

"Stay close, okay? And take your phone."

"There's no service," Tobi said.

"Try the Wi-Fi, it's on the map we just got."

"I already tried it. It sucks."

I knew better than to challenge them on that point. As the resident tween, Tobi could find Wi-Fi in ten seconds. I wondered if this would be the case in every stupid KOA. They were set up to vacation and get away from it all, not trying to survive outdoors because everything indoors had suddenly become potentially fatal. It was our first night out and I already missed being in. I wanted my TV and a couch. I wanted to watch the news. I wanted a hotel.

I noticed Tobi had not moved. "Leash up the dogs, please." The edge was back. Tobi gave me a defensive *I am!* and was then pulled out of the RV by the excited dogs.

◆ ◆ ◆

Martha appeared at the window and handed me the keys. Her head-lamp blinded me as she gave me stern instructions. "Here's what I want you to do. When I say *go*, slowly, slowly pull forward. And I will tell you when to stop. Okay? Follow my go."

Her "go." She's such a stage manager. Giving actors firm and clear instructions like "go" is a regular thing. As an actor who is also her wife, I can get annoyed when we fall into the actor/stage manager roles, but in the interest of getting along after a grueling day, I agreed.

She went back into the darkness and Tobi came back with the dogs after too short of a walk, telling me they were creeped out by the darkness. We'd wanted to arrive in the light, but the sun had set hours earlier. We'd left in plenty of time and even had the time change in our favor, but a detour to see the world's largest rocking chair and the world's largest ball of yarn had left us hours behind schedule. Six hours behind schedule.

I started the loud RV engine—much louder than my normal car, which was a sensible Honda currently parked in my brother's driveway in Cincinnati.

"Tobs, I am going to move," I said. "Take a seat."

They sat right down on the floor. The dogs happily flopped down next to them.

Martha gave me the ready.

"On my count. Three, two, one, go! Slowly!" I put the RV in drive and started to inch forward. The silverware rattled in its drawer.

"Good, good . . ." I could feel the RV rise up on the right side. Something heavy fell in the back. I imagined it was the suction-cupped shampoo bottle.

"Almost there . . .stop!" I stopped and heard a pop. The RV banged down on the right side. I leaned out the window.

"What happened?"

"No big deal," Martha said. "You went a little too far. Try it again." I started to go.

"Wait! Not yet. I have to reset!" I threw the RV into park and jumped out, tripping over a tree root as I went to the back.

"Martha, you know I can't see you or hear you. I could run over you for all I know. Please, *please* make sure I can see you in my rear-view mirror."

She nodded. "Yup, sure."

I stomped back to the cab and climbed in.

Tobi appeared in the shadows. "Mom. You seem stressed."

This was Tobi's new favorite phrase. *You seem stressed.*

Ya think? I'd just lost the best job of my life in a global pandemic and was trying to level a gigantic RV when I'd much, much, much rather be checking into a Westin.

"I'm okay." I told them. "Really."

They looked at me suspiciously. "Mom. I can tell when you are stressed. Talk to me. You know I love you more than anything."

Poor Tobi. This sweet kid whose life had been thrown upside down. They were always right there, loving me. For as long as Tobi could talk, they'd regaled me with love, usually saying, "Mom. Mom. Guess what?"

"What?"

"I love you. Did you know that?"

And then five minutes later, "Mom. Mom. Guess what? I still love you."

Charlotte had forever lamented over how annoying it was that Tobi told me they loved me so much. "We get it. You love her. Geez." Speaking for myself, it's awesome. And to be fair, even when Tobi used it as a tool to calm me down—like right now—it worked.

I turned around and made eye contact, trying to think of a fun job. "How about if you start to pull out the stuff for the s'mores?" I asked. "It's in a box in the cabinet above the door."

"Sure!"

I learned quickly that s'mores over a campfire fixes most upsets. Martha appeared in the rear-view mirror. "Can you see me?"

"I can. Thank you."

"Ok. Let's do it again."

After six tries, I finally managed to balance the RV on the stack of orange plastic levelers, and we all cheered. I had Tobi check the status of the RV with the golf ball I'd found in my dad's coat, which I'd pulled from my sister's basement just before we'd left. I didn't know what I'd do with that golf ball, but I figured I'd at least like to have it along with me. Dad had been the traveler in the family.

"The ball is steady," Tobi announced in a loud voice.

Now to build the first-ever campfire.

◆ ◆ ◆

Tobi had proved to be a campsite savant, knowing how to build a fire, and nestling right in with their telescoping hot dog skewer. Tobi had camped many times with their dad, and they were proud to still know how to do it all. We deferred to their expertise quite a bit, and heaped on praise, which made them happy. Martha and I had never camped, so the praise was real. It was fun to see my kid be excited, after weeks of hating online school. Nothing made me happier than to see Tobi confident. We all felt the freedom of the moment. "Tobi, you're nailing it!" Martha bellowed in the silent campground. We both told her to hush. I was happy to see Martha happy, too. She'd had some unexpected work creep up during the final days of packing and it had eaten away at her time and some of her joy about the trip. She now had to work as we drove, and sometimes we had to stop and find Wi-Fi signals for her Zoom meetings and rehearsals. This was sometimes a bummer, but she tried to stay positive.

After a good campfire, the first night was rough. We'd discovered Dot had peed on the bed just as we were going to bed the night before. Tobi had spent most of that first day lounging on our bed as we drove, unable to sit on the couch because Desi the eighty-five-pound golden retriever was taking up the whole thing. The floor was hot, and Desi, covered in fur, wasn't having it. Tobi happily played Animal Crossing in the back, on our bed, to avoid all of the cross animals in the RV. I assumed Tobi had spilled a drink on our bed, so when I'd climbed in, exhausted, smelling like campfire smoke, I'd yelled to them when my hand landed in a giant wet spot.

"What did you spill on our bed? It's soaking wet!"

They stuck their head out of the curtains they'd pulled shut. "Nothing."

"Well, something was spilled." I sounded accusatory because I was accusatory. I was over it. I was over everything. "This day can't get any worse."

I stuck my nose in the wet spot and took a deep whiff, so I could remind Tobi of exactly what they had spilled based on the scent, and got a deep wave of cat urine.

"DAMN IT. Martha!"

Martha was outside, doing all the outside chores that I was trying to avoid. We'd decided my job was interior, her job was exterior. I wanted any job that avoided the dumping of the pee and poop, and since Dot had peed, even though it was inside, I decided it was Martha's terrain. Besides, Dot was Martha's cat from her life before me, and she was proprietary about all things Dot-related, much as

I was about my kids. Generally speaking, the division of labor was kid care = me, animal care = Martha. So, I was in the clear to get Martha on this inside job.

I stuck my head out the RV door and loudly whispered her name. I could see her headlamp bobbing around the fire pit. "Martha."

She came over, blinding me. I reached up and lowered her lamp. "Dot peed on the bed."

"I'm sure it wasn't Dot. Maybe Sparky?" She looked down. "Oh shit, Ethel's out again. You have to keep an eye on her. This is the third time she's run out. Earlier she climbed out the driver's side door and I found her balancing on the side-view mirror."

Fortunately, Ethel was quite rotund, so her waddle was easy to spot with Martha's handy headlamp. "You really should put on a headlamp. It's a *game changer*," Martha said. She had a passion for headlamps.

I did not. They were ugly.

Martha scooped up Ethel and came in. "God, that air conditioner is loud." It was. I was also hot. I knew what was coming next. Martha reached up and switched it off. "That's better."

"I'm burning up," I said, annoyed. "Come in here and see the bed."

Martha felt it with her whole hand, palm down. "It's wet alright. Maybe Tobi spilled something?"

The curtains ripped open. "I didn't. I already said that." Every time Tobi popped their head out from the overhead cab, Sparky went nuts. Whining and crying, he wanted to get up there. "Can I please have Sparky up here?"

"No," Martha and I said in unison. I went on, "He has no way down." I added, "Sorry, honey" in hopes it would soften the blow. The curtains snapped shut.

Martha started sniffing, first her palm and then nose deep in the covers. "Cat pee, for sure."

I wanted to roll my eyes or say I told you so but didn't, which, given my mood, was a feat.

She started pulling the covers up. "Soaked all the way through."

"Even the egg crate?" I was aghast, my night's sleep evaporating before my eyes. We had no extra sheets, no extra anything. I'd splurged on the egg crate after a lot of searching for the best but cheapest brand and I couldn't believe the cat had ruined it. I was so tired I contemplated sleeping on the bed despite the pee, but it was impossible. The pee smell alone was too strong. I started ripping everything off the bed, totally over it.

"GREAT." Rip. "PERFECT." Rip. "AWESOME." Rip. "So far everything is going just great."

Martha started to help, trying to calm me down. "Okay, now, okay."

It was no one's fault but I wanted to blame someone anyway. "Just leave it. I'll do it." I bundled it all up, stomped out the door, keeping Ethel at bay with my foot, and threw the massive pee pile, egg crate and all, on a picnic table.

Martha looked at me as I stomped back in. "Did you spread it out to dry?"

"Dry? NO. It's trashed. I'm throwing it out in the trash."

"I can spray it with Nature's Miracle and . . ."

"It's TRASH."

"Fine. Whatever you say."

Martha went back outside, and I heard the back storage compartment open, and her looking for something. I knew she was going out to spray the bedding and stretch it out over the picnic table to dry. I knew that was the right thing to do. I knew I was being completely unreasonable. This kept happening to me during Covid-19. Things I could normally deal with became overwhelming. My skin was too thin; the pandemic had worn it away layer by layer.

I had to salvage it. The bedding might be trash, but most of the first day had not been. I made the bed with some extra sleeping beds Maryday had shoved in at the last minute—God bless her—and made it all ready for sleep. I made a spectacularly crabby but very funny video for Maryday, lamenting all the reasons an RV was a terrible idea, and sent it off. And then I put in some ear plugs and slept not well, but better than I imagined I would. Point scored for the RV. The bed was pretty cozy.

Martha, unfortunately, did not sleep well. Unbeknownst to me, she spent most of the night sitting up with Dot, who had fallen down the RV steps. In the morning Martha was visibly upset. "She's blind and so old. This is terrible for her."

Tobi had the best sleep of all, declaring, "Best sleep ever!" After a long and lazy stretch, they piled on top of Desi for a cuddle, asking, "What's for breakfast?"

I took my first shower, and the water was surprisingly hot and strong enough to rinse my thick hair. Martha had sprayed the egg crate and, in the sun, it had dried up. She sniffed it thoroughly and declared it "Clean!" I apologized to everyone for my grumpiness the night before, promised to do better, made some strong coffee, and started to pack up to leave. Martha dumped the tanks and when I asked her how it was, she reported, "Uneventful. Easy."

At least something had gone well.

The only thing that was a real and obvious issue was Dot, and I could see it in Martha's eyes. Martha looked at me and said, "I'm not sure how Dot is going to do this. First peeing on the bed and then yowling all night. Not good."

I agreed with her. It wasn't good. We pulled out for Oklahoma City and set the only goal as making it before dark.

CHAPTER 8

ONE CUP

One cup.

She makes coffee one cup at a time.

Finding each other—me, a woman married to a man for twenty years, and her, an out and proud single woman—was a journey that surprised me at every turn.

There were things about her I wanted to change, like her penchant for using milk crates and cardboard boxes as storage. Functional? Yes. Ugly? Yes. She was fifty, yet her apartment looked like a dorm room decorated with street finds. Other people's recycling was her Pottery Barn.

My home was a breezy and sparse Southern California 70s ranch with a pool. I had matching mugs and a white leather couch. I had citrus floral throw pillows. It was intentional.

My house was furnished for a family of four; hers was furnished for a lesbian bachelor. But the "one-cup." I marveled at the "one-cup."

The first time I slept in her L-shaped studio, after a night of lovemaking that blew away any notion that a shared-gender sexual experience might be less than, she made me coffee.

I was still absorbing what had happened, still marveling at the person I'd discovered inside my same skin, and still tangled up in covers and guilt when Martha jumped out of bed with the statement: I will make coffee.

In my other life I was the coffee maker. Coffee is my friend, my comfort. That first sip is my favorite moment of any day. I discovered coffee when my child had colic and those ground beans led me through hazy days and nights of screaming. It ushered in weeks with my sick mother in Cincinnati, where I would make coffee lightened with Coffee Mate, something I never buy for myself but makes my coffee taste like Mom.

Most days I make Starbucks out of the bag, already ground, and my coffee pot makes it extra hot. The grounds ground me. It's delicious.

It's my first morning in Martha's apartment. I hear grinding from Martha's kitchen. She's making noises and having a conversation with her cat. She is loud, the cat is loud, the grinding is loud. I am quiet and comfortable. There is a loud whistle of a teapot.

"Are you making tea?" I ask.

She trots out of the kitchen. When she's happy, she trots.

"Do you want tea? I can make tea!"

Answering a question with a question is a pet peeve of mine, but I am too enamored to care.

"I love coffee. I was just wondering why you had the kettle on."

Maybe she has a French press. I have one too, buried somewhere in my white cabinets. It had its moment but the coffee it pressed proved to be both crunchy and quick to cool.

"I'm making us one-cuppers," she says, and disappears.

This. Was. Fascinating.

I get up, put on a bra, and walk into the kitchen to see what is happening.

She nearly fills her tiny kitchen, so I wrap myself around her from behind to see what's happening on the counter. A lot is happening. Spoons laid out on paper towels, a deep green plastic funnel resting on a small mug with a cat on it, a fox mug beside it, at the ready. She slowly pours hot water into the coffee-filled funnel. As we wait for it to drain, we kiss.

◆ ◆ ◆

"You put a bra on?" she asks.

"I always wear a bra."

"In the house? We'll change that."

I laugh. I know I'll always wear a bra, but I'm interested in this different coffee.

"Talk me through this. What's happening here?"

"This is a one cup. You've never had this? It's delicious!"

She throws her head back and yells "it's delicious" so loudly that I belly laugh. I am delighted by her passion in every way, especially for this multi-step coffee, which is (by definition) one cup short of how much coffee I drink in the morning.

"What kind of coffee is this?"

"This is the most delicious coffee. I buy it across the street at Empire Coffee, which is locally owned. This is—" She looks at the bag. "Obama blend. Smell the beans."

I stick my nose in the open bag. It smells good, like coffee. Starbucks smells good, too.

She repeatedly pours hot water into the small paper filter, and we watch as the water slowly, so slowly, drains into the mug. As she pours, she talks. A morning person. Huh.

I mention if I were single, I might have a Keurig, and am told about the *Keurig cups in the landfill!* and the *wasted space on the counter!*

I am converted. I am in love. I think about how I sometimes used two Keurig cups if I had a large mug, but I do not mention it. My carbon footprint is Bigfoot.

She removes the funnel from the mug, hands the mug to me, and dumps the used paper filter in the sink. Then she starts from the top. One cup number two.

I stand and hold my coffee, reeling in the differences. The many mornings I'd spent hustling into the kitchen to switch on the preset coffee pot before waking up my children. My then-husband showering for work. The dog peeing in the yard. Breakfasts are made, headlines are watched, lunches and backpacks are filled. And then we leave the house with different kids in different cars and different travel mugs of coffee.

I wait politely for her cup to be completed, though I worry mine will get cold. "I'll be quick," she says. She wants to drink the coffee together. I kiss her again. I haven't even brushed my teeth.

Once she's finished one cup of coffee, we drink number two on her hand-me-down couch and watch boats float by on the Hudson from twenty-four floors up. I am happy to dock.

Later, Martha and I get a fancy coffee pot as a wedding present. We move into a bigger apartment. We have new furniture now, but I now recognize and save "terrific" boxes for Martha to marvel over and use. My carbon footprint is smaller. My children love Martha's passions. She trots for them, too, making lunches.

We now have two "one-cuppers" safely snuggled in our cabinet, retired but always at the ready.

CHAPTER 9

CANYONS

"I'm sick of Diana, the Princess of Wales, being in the RV with us," I whispered in Martha's direction for the umpteenth time. "And the entire Royal Family, if I'm being honest." She shushed me and shoved her AirPods further in her ears, squinting at the road as she drove.

I looked out the window, mad. Oklahoma was flat and boring, and I couldn't even complain about it because I was supposed to be quiet. Martha's show *Diana the Musical* was in rehearsals for upcoming show changes, all of which were happening on Zoom and in this RV. On this particular day she was in a meeting that required her to listen in, but not participate, so she drove and listened at the same time. Not ideal, but necessary.

Even in my bad mood I had to admit that she looked cute, all hunched over the steering wheel, her eyebrows knitted together, deep in concentration. Her show was new, extremely hard, and she was the boss. By continuing with the RV trip, her other team of stage managers had to seriously pick up her slack when we were out of service, and she felt terrible about it. But she'd promised me she would drive Tobi across the country, in direct conflict with stage-managing a massive musical on Zoom. The other problem was simply the act of driving all these miles. Martha and I had made a deal before we started on the trip that she'd do most of the driving. She was the one who had a fantasy about being a cement truck driver, not me. I wasn't terribly confident driving this gajillion-pound house eighty miles an hour down the highway. The addition of *Diana* complicated things.

I wished it was me working. So did Martha. I wished I was more comfortable driving the RV. So did Martha.

◆ ◆ ◆

There are a zillion funny Zoom stories about people who thought they were muted and went to the bathroom, or some guy who stood up and wasn't wearing pants. But rehearsals on Zoom are a special kind of hell, especially for a musical. Remember as a kid when you'd sing *Row Row Row Your Boat* and then you'd sing it in a round? Like your music teacher said, "Okay, Suzie, you start, and then William, you join in on the next part, and then Zeek, you join in on the third part? And it will all sound SO COOL?" But as soon as William starts singing Zeek is like, wait, I think I should go now, and then Suzie starts to sing William's part and then it sounds like cats screeching all at different times and volumes?

That's what a Zoom music rehearsal sounds like. Even when you are dealing with some of the best voices on Broadway.

Smart people in the audio and music departments eventually figured out how to do it, but it was never great and never satisfying. Like it or not, it was happening, and Martha had to appear. Her feelings on the matter were clear. "Around the world theater is on pause but somehow *Diana* the musical is still rehearsing. I'm happy for the work, but, you know, I was excited to just drive around and look out the RV window."

I was mad that she was in rehearsal, but I was madder that it wasn't *me* in rehearsal. I'd happily Zoom into a music rehearsal just so I could feel hope and purpose and community and get a paycheck. If *Come From Away* had called me, I would have turned that rig around, illegally driven it into Manhattan, and parked on 45th Street outside our stage door. No. Questions. Asked. For me, the entire pandemic was nothing but treading water until I got the call to go back to work. Each Broadway delay laid me out in a new depression. And I mean that literally. I would stay in bed the entire next day, the optimistic wind knocked out of me. *I don't know how we will survive this* became the headline in my head.

For Martha, it was a totally different circumstance. She is an in-demand stage manager who goes from show to show to show. Martha took the pandemic as a chance to do all the things she'd dreamed of doing after years in a windowless rehearsal room. She wanted to roll the windows down, take a back road through mid-America farm country, and enjoy the view.

Getting Martha to the best cell reception possible was a constant job. We'd pick up a free local Wi-Fi signal so she could appear on camera.

Her company would tease her in the early moments of these meetings, "Where are you now, Martha?"

"Today I am Zooming in from a McDonald's parking lot," she'd say. "Near Flagstaff."

Or "Next to a Starbucks. In Joshua Tree." Or "Outside a Cracker Barrel in Yuma." We went wherever free Wi-Fi was served.

Others were also Zooming in from afar. Many people moved home with their parents. And not just young people, people in their forties and fifties who were living with their elderly parents. Sometimes taking care of them, often with children in tow. Martha Zooming in from an RV was simply, in 2020, par for the course.

Free Wi-Fi was listed on most RV websites, but we came to realize quickly that RV park Wi-Fi was designed for a quick email check-in.

It was *not* designed for 2020 when everyone and their brother was trying to work in their RVs, needing to Zoom. The streaming load on the RV park Wi-Fi signal made the speed and reliability akin to the dial-up AOL we had in the 90s. Super crappy.

By the time we finally reached the Grand Canyon on day four, we were all excited. I drove that leg of the trip, which was not on a highway, but instead on a beautiful pine-tree-lined road that climbed in altitude. Tobi and Sparky sat up front with me, Desi lounged on the couch, Dot slept fitfully in her Amazon box in the dinette, and Martha listened in to a meeting from the back, accompanied by Ethel, who claimed our bed during the drives. Martha finished her meeting just as we pulled up to the ranger station at the entrance. This was our first national park stay, and it felt different from our other stays immediately. And, not to brag, but we managed to get there before dark, the first time we'd managed that. I was greeted by a ranger.

"Welcome to the Grand Canyon. Are you camping or visiting?"

"Camping. Trailer Village RV Park. For two nights. Pull through, full hookups." I had the lingo down. This was also our first two-night stay, and it had practically taken selling a kidney to reserve it. The Grand Canyon had just opened after the Covid-19 shutdown, and I'd pounced on the website to secure a spot. I'd had a lot of practice working government phone and internet systems in the pandemic while registering for unemployment, so getting a competitive campsite reservation was in my wheelhouse. The ranger looked at our reservation, gave me a map, and gave us the latest news.

"There is a wildfire up in the North Rim, so we are not allowing fire of any kind right now. And it might be a little hazy for you with the smoke and all, but it's still beautiful. Have a good time."

He was so nonchalant about the fire situation. A wildfire? Isn't that a big deal? I mean, wild is right there in the title. But he seemed chill so I acted chill and passed that chill onto everyone else and so we drove on in, as if driving headfirst into a wildfire was something I did every day of the week.

Martha immediately took the map and started navigating to the campground. I am more of a "feel my way" kind of a person, so I ignored her, following signs to get as close to the canyon as fast as I could. For all I knew, the park would close due to wildfires or Covid-19 or whatever in the hell else 2020 had to offer, so it seemed fair to cut to the chase, just in case. See the view, hookup later.

I followed the wide road to a lookout called Mather Point, noting the lack of traffic, especially the absence of shuttle buses. The park was a ghost town. We were one of about a dozen vehicles in a parking lot made for hundreds of cars.

I asked Martha, "Do you think this is Covid-19 or wildfires?"

She shrugged her response. "Both?"

We got out and decided to enjoy the canyon view while we had it. It was grand, so to speak. But also, a little eerie to be somewhere so vast and yet feel seemingly alone. What should have felt peaceful instead felt like an apocalypse. Our friend Ellen sometimes sent pictures of the empty avenues in New York City saying, "Where are all the people?" I wanted to send a picture back to say, "Well, they aren't here!"

We went to the campsite and found our spot, relieved to see other people in the park, including many Cruise America RVs, our first Cruise America sightings. It was oddly soothing, since we sometimes wondered if we were the only people out renting an RV during this time. This started a theme that would continue the rest of the trip, where Martha would honk and wave every time we saw a Cruise America RV. It reminded me of when we first got together, and I noticed she'd nod to any outward-appearing lesbian on the street.

I'd asked, "What is that thing you're doing? Is it like a secret lesbian handshake or something?" And she gave me the nod and said, "That's right. We've got to see each other. Stick together." Now it was the Cruise America car honk and wave. Martha likes to be part of a pack.

We started the multi-hour process of unpacking all the crap we'd packed the night before to ready ourselves for the two-night stay in the Grand Canyon. Martha was getting faster at the hookups outside, and I was getting faster at unpacking the interior essentials. I was trying to manage my horrible mood, which I couldn't seem to shake. I criticized everything.

"Who tied the dogs up by the door? I am completely tangled up!"

"The ice trays are overfilled!"

I got into the habit of sending Maryday daily videos and they always started exactly the same way. "I don't get it. Who thought this would be fun?" She would howl with laughter, which helped.

We had shopped to grill and were pretty bummed out about the no fire rule, but if we'd mastered anything in this weird year, it was how to change our plans at a moment's notice whether we wanted to or not. The RV had a nice little kitchen, which we had not previously utilized, so I cooked up some veggie burgers and corn and served it on the picnic table just as darkness came. We looked at the stars and ate in the pitch black. The candles on the table, the feel of the altitude, and the beauty of the park all felt new and different than any other stop.

Tobi declared it the "best meal yet." I was grateful and pulled sweet Tobi in for a long snuggle.

"Guess what? I love you, Mom."

"I love you, too, kid."

I was about to lose them for the summer. Something I didn't talk about, but I was thinking about it all the time. At least with Tobi there I had a solid job to do. Once the drop-off happened, I'd be out of work, no longer a parent on a need-by-need basis, and I'd be stuck in the rig with Martha, the Royal Family, and the pets.

The next morning, I wanted some time with Tobi, so we jumped on bikes for a mommy/child day while Martha worked. The Grand Canyon has a series of bike trails, which seemed like an easy way to get to the little village from our RV park. Considering that we were in an RV with no other car, it was the only way to get around unless we completely unhooked, which we did not want to do. It wasn't as perfect a time as I'd pictured in my imagination when I pulled the bikes off the back of the RV; Tobi was nervous on a bike that felt too big, and I was impatient.

I looked at Tobi once we'd finally parked and apologized. "I'm sorry I'm such a crab."

Tobi shrugged their shoulders and said, "It's OK. I'm in a bad mood, too."

We shook on it. Bad moods unite.

I outlined my terrible mood in great detail in my journal. I won't keep going with journal entries both because they are embarrassingly narcissistic and because I simply got too busy to even keep a journal soon after this. But this entry is a pretty good snapshot of my state of mind on day five of our trip.

June 17, 2020 Wednesday

I am such a grump which is ridiculous given that I am in this most beautiful place and doing everything as planned. Right this moment I am sitting on a bench looking at the view with Tobi right next to me drawing a tree.

This beautiful Instagram picture moment would not really reflect the upset I feel inside.

My job. I miss my job.

This should be a two-show day.

There is a raven watching me. Are they a vulture? Do they feast on dead dreams?

Kidding.

Maybe one will take a few of the pets.

Kidding.

Kinda.

Ethel and I are sharing a mood. She wants OUT. She meows and scratches at the door and windows constantly. For such an old and fat cat she is shockingly spry.

Jesus H she gets out a lot.

Somewhere my dad is cheering her on. He said she shared his claustrophobia.

Dot isn't good.

Disoriented.

Bloody pee.

Martha thinks she is improving.

I feel awful for her.

For both of them.

Desi had car sickness and threw up three times, once in my purse.

That was awesome.

Meanwhile, Sparky is totally fine. RVing suits him. Much to bark at and smell.

The Grand Canyon sure is beautiful. Wow.

I worry about all the money I am spending. I really under-estimated the cost of gas. It's $100+ every time we fill up, even with the cheap gas this summer.

Then the campground costs—anywhere from $35-80 per night.

And the RV rental is over $100 per day.

I've lost my mind.

We have to cut down costs.

Shorter trips/cheaper campsites.

Just talked to a huge family of blondes who told me all about how Covid is a myth.

I hope Broadway is back by this fall.

Tobi leaves soon for the summer.

Don't think about that.

I need something good to happen. A sign.

◆ ◆ ◆

The smoke smell in the campground was more present on the second day—enough that I checked in with a ranger. She assured me the wildfire was far away and would be contained. "It's a little rough for the animals that live up there, but hopefully it'll be over soon."

We packed up the RV as best as we could and went to the nearby town of Tusayan, Arizona. While Martha found some Wi-Fi in a McDonald's parking lot to attend another unconscious bias training meeting, Tobi and I ordered Mexican takeout from a little family restaurant called Playa Bonita. They seemed as grateful for the business as I was for their delicious chicken enchiladas.

We went back to the Canyon, watched the sunset, watched *Ratatouille*, and went to bed.

At six in the morning Martha and I woke up to a loud squeaking sound. I assumed it was Ethel rubbing her paws in her plastic litter box, a normal sound in our animal planet. I rolled over and closed my eyes to go back to sleep. The RV rocked from side to side, as it did whenever anyone rolled over in our house on wheels.

But this time when I rolled over and rocked our world, the rocking didn't stop.

Nor did the squeaking sound.

"Mar. What is that?"

"I don't know."

We laid and listened to it for a minute, feeling the rocking movement, which lined up with the squeak.

Squeak/rock/squeak/rock.

I sat up on my elbows and looked around.

"It sounds so close!" I said. "It sounds like it is coming from outside your window."

I climbed over her as she slid open the curtains and right there, so close that we could touch it, was a giant brown head with large ears resembling a horse. And that giant brown animal was licking the side of our RV right under Martha's window. Its tongue was creating the squeaking sound as it licked and licked. It appeared to be licking the area right where the hose was screwed into the water tank.

"Is that a horse?" I whispered.

"It's an elk."

"Why is it licking our RV?"

Martha thought for a minute, and then got up to check. "I forgot to turn off the water pump when we hooked up to the campsite water."

"Don't turn it off yet, this little guy is so thirsty. Let him drink."

We watched in silence, in awe. I took a video because, you know, if you don't film it, did it really happen? That elk licked and licked and licked. The dogs, who bark at everything, slept soundly.

I sneaked over and woke up Tobi because if you don't wake up your kid for a wild animal adventure in a national park, are you really a parent?

It was incredible. He was so close we could see the inside of his ears and we could see his little black nose wrinkle up as he drank. We could see every single eyelash. And he could see us, but he didn't care. He drank.

I was in awe, Martha was in awe, Tobi was in awe. I'd worked so hard to make everything perfect that I'd forgotten the most memorable moments can be found by mistake. We climbed out of the RV and watched as more and more elk walked by, so near we could touch them.

I looked at Mar and Tobi and said, "My dad would be flipping out right now. I can't believe he's not here to see this. Listen to them calling to each other, do you hear it?" We listened to the distinct call of the elk, the parents to their babies, telling them, I imagined, that it was safe. To come out and drink.

Soon the campground was overrun with herds of thirsty elk. People started putting out pans of water, filling coolers, anything to help the elk. We all ran around, astounded by the majesty of the moment, but sad about the cause. We united as we socially distanced, focused on one goal. Save the elk.

And then it hit me.

Tobi was my elk, and I was protecting them from harm. That's what the RV trip was all about. Not my comfort, not Martha's *Diana* job, but Tobi and the virus and delivering them safely. And now, as we were getting closer to drop-off time, I was not grumpy, I was not hating the RV, I was just sad to say goodbye.

I kissed Tobi's face all over and said, "I am going to miss you, so much, kid."

"Yeah. I like you, too." And then a smile.

I'd do anything for that little smile.

Later that night, I sent Maryday the video of the elk and the text *All worth it. Staying out forever.*

CHAPTER 10

CALIFORNIA

Dot was in trouble. I looked at Martha as she sat on the sofa in the San Diego apartment we were living in for ten days. She needed excellent Wi-Fi while she finished up the final and most critical days of *Diana*. Giant tears rolled down her face.

"This is a disaster," she said. "I can't have Dot suffer like this."

The drive from Cincinnati had been a roller coaster for all of us, but it had been pure misery for Dot. Martha had devised a little house for her out of an Amazon box, and we'd kept her safely boxed in the dinette while driving. She rarely left her box now and had started to pee inside it. Her fur was matted, and she smelled. Martha sniffed her and shook her head. "This is never a good sign. She's not washing herself."

Martha's rearing of Dot was exemplary, and, as she often said, Dot was her longest relationship. It was everyone's second question to Martha. Question one, "How are you?" Question two, "How is Dot?" Martha had been gearing up for Dot's death for years, wishing she'd go peacefully in her sleep, but it seemed we were at a breaking point. After twenty-one years of great cat care, Martha felt it was time to put Dot down.

Because I'd previously lived in San Diego for three years and had my own small posse of pets, I had an excellent vet. This was important because Martha loved and respected Dot's vet in New York City. To be away from their trusted vet in the final moments was additionally upsetting for Martha. I couldn't do a lot for Dot, but I could pull strings with my local vet. I called the office and made an appointment. Martha cried as she carried Dot in her Amazon box out to the car, the box with an untimely smiley face on it. We'd rented a car for the few days we were in San Diego to relieve ourselves from running every errand in the RV, which was parked in the empty parking lot of the La Jolla Playhouse. I had to admit, I kind of missed it. Me liking an RV. Who'da thunk.

The vet's office told me to call them when we arrived, not to come into the office. The pandemic had started to spread west, and California businesses were mostly closed. The office was open, but also not. We didn't really understand how it would work.

We pulled up and Martha called the receptionist, who instructed us to pull the car around to the back of the building and to bring Dot to the second door. She said someone would be waiting for us. Everything in Southern California is in a strip mall, so once we figured out how to get back there, we saw a fully masked and suited-up vet hospital worker waiting for us. There were other cars parked as well, with masked people and their pets. I watched from the car as Martha approached the worker. They talked for a minute, then Martha handed her the box, which the worker took in the building. Martha, a chatterer, talked to a couple nearby who were holding a Yorkie. They looked hot.

The sun beat down and heated my bare legs through the windshield. I wondered if I was getting sunburned despite the thick glass. If we'd been in the RV I could have made an iced coffee while we waited. Or taken a shower.

Martha finally got back in the car, sweating, and explained what was going on. "They won't let anyone in. We have to sit here and wait while Dot is being examined, then the doctor will call us."

I'd imagined going into the office with Martha and Dot, and I'd tend to Martha as the vet tended to Dot. Instead, we listened to *Marketplace* on NPR with the AC blasting and waited for the phone to ring. We watched as the Yorkie was led inside, the owners standing near the door, unsure of what to do. I could see the guy fanning himself and was tempted to ask them if they wanted to wait in the cool car with us, but then I remembered the reason we were all outside to begin with and thought better of it.

When the vet called I could only hear Martha's side of the conversation, but her face said it all. "Mmm hmm . . . Yes . . . Okay . . . I understand . . . Yes, I would . . . No, I don't think so . . . Can I think about that for a minute?"

She hung up and looked at me. "She has kidney failure, no doubt about it. It's time." She put her head in her hands. "I can't be in there with her."

"So, what happens to her?"

"They're bringing her back out so I can say goodbye. They gave me the option of holding her while they inject her, but . . ." She looked around the parking lot. "Where would they do it? There isn't even any shade. They should put up a pop tent or something." We watched as the Yorkie's parents huddled in the doorway and I wondered what was going on. I had a feeling I knew.

Dot and Martha had to do this together. And as weird as I thought it all was, I really couldn't have an opinion. "Honey, what are you planning to do?" I braced myself. I was pretty sure I was about to witness a driveway euthanasia.

"I am not going to hold Dot in the back of a strip mall parking lot in the blazing sun while they put her down," Martha said clearly. "That is too much for even me. I will go and say goodbye and let them take her inside. That's what I'm doing."

"Do you want me to come?" I asked.

"Nope. Thank you. I've got this." She opened the car door and looked at me. "2020 is so damn weird."

Martha said her goodbyes while I watched through the rearview mirror. When she got back in the car, she told me she was opting for cremation, but we would not pick up her ashes. Martha already had the ashes of two cats, Mama and Wishon, in our apartment in New York. Her decision not to pick up Dot was a practical one.

"I don't want to carry around Dot's ashes in an RV, where would we even put her? I opted for her to have a group burial at sea."

I laughed. "Are you serious? A group burial at sea? What does that mean?"

"I don't know. I guess it means they take all of the cremated remains of the latest pets and dump them in the ocean."

"Seriously?"

"I'm just guessing. It sounds nice, though."

I wondered if the Yorkie would be on the boat, too.

We waited a long time in the parking lot. Finally, when forty-five minutes or so had gone by, I asked her, "What happens now?"

She wasn't sure. "I think they'll call. Don't you think?"

We waited some more. Finally, Martha called the office. She spoke with them and then looked at me and said, "Well, she's gone. Turns out they did it right away. They just forgot to call."

We sat for a minute more. Then she said, "You want to get a coffee?" So we drove through the Starbucks in the strip mall. As we drove home Martha said, "I am surprised I'm not sadder. But I guess I know Dot was ready."

When we dropped off Tobi, we'd also dropped off Desi, so now we were down from two adults, one child, two dogs, and two cats to two adults, one dog, and one cat. With so much room to spare in the empty nest of our RV, I decided to fill it up. While Martha finished up her rehearsals for *Diana*, I headed to an old storage unit of mine, deep in the California desert.

◆ ◆ ◆

In total, Martha and I had four storage units between us. Martha loves her storage units and will never empty them. I, on the other hand, was anxious to empty mine out and save $76 a month. I deduced that whatever was in there had been there for four years and I most certainly no longer needed it. The plan was to dump it.

But then I got there and realized I'd rolled the door down on things I loved. I had an entire set of Log Cabin dishware and whether I needed it in my current life, I wanted it. It was from Macy's and had been a gift from my mother over several Christmases, starting in 2001. She'd told me at the time it was important for two reasons: 1) It looked like my favorite book cover, *Little House in the Big Woods* and 2) It looked like the log cabin I'd bought just north of New York City where we'd lived for about a year after 9/11.

And there was more important stuff in there that I'd forgotten about. I had set pieces from when *Cats* closed on Broadway at the Winter Garden Theater; I was part of the cast when the show closed, and we were given free rein to pick things out. I had a giant tooth-paste tube and a paintbrush from what was called "The Junkyard," but I couldn't junk it. I had all the kids' favorite toys. There was a leather ottoman from Crate and Barrel. There was beautiful artwork. I couldn't trash this stuff—that was impossible! And I knew just what to do.

◆ ◆ ◆

The RV had a hilariously huge back storage area that I called the basement and Martha called the garage, about which we corrected each other like two old biddies.

"I am putting the grill back in the basement."

"I think you mean garage."

"You mean garage, I mean basement."

"Whatever."

This is what spending twenty-four hours a day in a rolling home does to people. Whatever we wanted to call it, it was now my new storage U-Haul. Martha wasn't so sure.

"Sharon, we can't just load up the RV with a bunch of crap. It's too heavy."

Martha was always freaking out about weight. We'd watched Lucy and Desi's comedy *The Long, Long Trailer* before we'd left Cincinnati, to laugh at all the funny things that could go wrong. This was a mistake. Martha kept bringing it up—she'd watched it not as a comedy, but as a documentary. As a cautionary tale. She was obsessed with the tanks. She'd talk about how heavy gas was. She'd bring up the thirty-gallon water tank. The contents of my storage unit were the final straw.

"Remember how Lucy kept hiding all the rocks in the trailer and Desi couldn't understand why the trailer was rolling backwards down the mountain?"

"Martha, it was a movie, and I am not hiding anything from you. We're talking about a couple of paintings and a few dishes."

"What about the books and toys?"

"Okay, yes, some."

"And an ottoman."

"We'll *use* the ottoman *in* the RV when we watch TV! You'll be able to put your feet up! What is your problem? When else will I have a huge vehicle that we are driving across the country? When will we ever have the time to do this?"

My idea was fantastic. I had to make it happen. I made my voice serious.

"Martha, it justifies the expense of the RV."

"Okay," she said, relenting, "But please, be careful."

Game, set, match. I figured I could hide some stuff and she'd never know how much was really in there. While she finished up rehearsals, I packed us up to leave San Diego, shoving my secret stash here, there, and everywhere. Lucy for the win.

With no kids to take care of and no jobs to go to, Martha and I were anchorless. We didn't really know where we wanted to go. I wanted to camp in state parks. "It'll be romantic. Just the two of us in the dark. We can build fires and look at the stars."

Besides, we had all this cool RV *stuff* to use. We'd spent weeks in Cincinnati going to Goodwill stores and Walmarts, with me agonizing over things like which tablecloth was the cutest for the overall RV design aesthetic. We each took great pains to find the perfect comfy chair, which were annoyingly non-matching, killing any shot at winning the HGTV RV design show in my head. But Martha needed a chair with a side table, and I wanted a high back, so design sacrifices were made. Martha bought things like adapters and hoses from some store called Harbor Freight, which she decreed the "Greatest Store Ever!!" I stuck to Target.

RVing, according to everyone, is dark. Like, when the sun goes down it's pitch black. We planned on doing a lot of off-the-grid camping, which meant a summer of stumbling around in the dark. I dedicated one entire cabinet to electric candles and batteries, wax candles, and matches. Martha found a torch-like flashlight she deemed "The Flame Thrower," which she'd turn on with a "wha-BAM" sound, lighting up faraway treetops. "If a bear sneaks up on us I'll hit it with a wha-BAM and scare it away."

In the garage/basement we had every kind of fire-starter and tools for grilling. We'd used it a couple of times in the first week with Tobi, but we'd been in a rush. Now, with the summer stretching out in front of us, I had priorities. I'd bought some grilling cookbooks and I wanted to get into it. I could imagine the delicious grub we could cook up now that I'd read about how to shove food into the embers. It was so Ma Ingalls on the Prairie. I could imagine my future cooking show, sponsored by Reynolds Wrap.

Martha had a different plan.

"Let's go see people!"

◆ ◆ ◆

Martha proudly says her only hobby is socializing. I remember early on in our relationship when a seasoned theater veteran named Shirley told Martha she was "The most gregarious stage manager I've ever met." On the other hand, despite the extroverted appearance of my job as an actress, when I am offstage, I can be surprisingly shy. If I were to describe Martha and me in terms of guests at a bed and breakfast, Martha would be the person who sits down at the breakfast table talking to everyone, swapping phone numbers, and laughing heartily. She can make everyone feel like they are her friend. I, on the other hand, would be more likely to ask if I could have my breakfast alone in my room. I will take my bed with my breakfast, please.

While I was packing up the last of the RV needs, Martha jumped on the phone with her best friend Jill whose family lives in a groovy compound in LA. She hung up, looked at me, and said with enthusiasm, "They can't wait to see us!"

I panicked. "Mar, we can't go inside."

I was constantly reminding her about Covid-19. This went all the way back to when we were packing the car to leave for Cincinnati in March; I ran into an actor near the parking garage and he asked me, "What's the matter with your wife? I just saw her, and she touched my face!"

When I confronted her about it, she explained he wasn't feeling well, so she was checking his head for fever.

Even Tobi noticed it and told me in St. Louis, "Mom, I don't mean to be a tattletale but Martha's outside talking to some guy, and she just shook hands with him." When Martha came home, Tobi greeted her at the door with hand sanitizer.

"Mom says you can't come in until you use this."

As time progressed and Covid-19 infections grew, Martha often thanked me.

"Thank God you got us out of New York. If it weren't for you, I would have stayed, hung out with friends, and come down with Covid-19 for sure." I had to agree. Martha and I had roles to play in the pandemic, and mine was always the Covid-19 police.

As we drove north to LA, Martha explained that Jill was as neurotic as I was about Covid-19 and insisted we come, but also insisted that we stay in the RV, parked on their street, and not come in the house. I was worried about parking our thirty-foot-long Airbnb on their very hilly street, but Martha said she and Jill had a spot where we could park. "It'll be great. Jill says it's flat enough for her van." We talked about how we could make it work. The RV had a generator we could run if we needed power, but it was loud and expensive. Martha ran to the store and bought a bright orange, fifty-foot outdoor extension cord.

"We don't have to plug in the whole RV," she explained, cord in hand. "All we need is enough power to plug in a light, our phones, and make coffee."

Our priorities. I wanted it on a t-shirt. *All I need is a light, my phone, and some coffee.*

"Doesn't it seem crappy to show up at people's houses and plug into their power? Isn't that expensive for them?"

Martha countered, "If we were staying in their house, we'd be using all kinds of power. Think of it that way. It's one extension cord. And we are still using our own bathroom and kitchen and everything else. It's a perfect combination. We see people but we don't have to stay in the house."

I had to agree, it was kind of genius. Martha continued. "People are starved to see other people. We are doing them a favor!" I wasn't sure I'd go quite that far, but it did sound like fun.

Also, I was excited to see Matt and Jill, who Martha had described as "totally rad" when she'd first taken me to meet them years before. Rad is not a word I use on any kind of regular basis or ever, but it perfectly describes Matt and Jill and their lifestyle and their kids. Martha was just as stoked. "We'll hang out with Matt and Jill in the back by the pool. It'll be amazing." Jill and Matt's pool overlooks Dodger Stadium, perched on top of a canyon. It's so LA you wouldn't believe it. I worried we'd never leave.

When we pulled up, Jill and Matt ran out and we all jumped around at the excitement of seeing each other. Jill is a chef and a planner extraordinaire. Matt, a film editor, is the kind of calm, friendly guy who spends his time curating the perfect playlist for guests. They owned a totally restored VW bus and loved to camp. They oooed and aahed at the massive size of our RV. "Epic!" Matt exclaimed. I oooed and aahed at how uneven their street was. I pointed it out to Martha and she agreed. "Yeah, I guess it's a little hillier than I'd remembered."

◆ ◆ ◆

The RV was parked precariously on the street at a severe angle. Like, if I put the golf ball down it would have rolled with such velocity it could have dented the dashboard.

After one miserable night of rolling into each other and tripping all over the RV, Matt and Jill overrode our determination to stay in our RV and put us in their guest house, despite my Covid-19 fears. Indoor plumbing and a flat bed. Rad. Still, as we lay in the guest house the first night, Martha whispered, "I feel like we are cheating on the RV." I agreed. I was excited to get back to it.

"Where are you guys heading next?" Jill asked. An innocent question that led to a total breakdown.

"We have no idea!" Martha laughed.

"You guys. California is THE BEST STATE," Jill said. "Go to Yosemite! Go to Big Sur!" She looked at Martha. "Have you ever been there? YOU MUST GO."

California state parks are notoriously impossible to book, and this year the capacity was cut by half. Jill was determined to make it work. "Everyone meet here in the morning. I'll make coffee."

We were all ready with our devices at 6:59 am, coffee in hand.

Jill did the countdown. "Ready? Dial! Log on!"

Matt did as he was told but he also wasn't sure what to do. "What do I do if they answer the phone?" I didn't know a single thing about California state parks and looked to Jill as she rattled off the ideal places to stay. Matt's eyes glazed over. "If someone answers I am just going to hand you the phone." He took a long drink of coffee.

Martha and I agreed. I was focusing more on the computer, hitting refresh to see if the parks opened up. After unemployment and then getting a spot at the Grand Canyon, this was getting to be a special skill for me. Suddenly, something opened up. "Two nights in Sequoia? Is that good?"

Martha slowly weighed it out loud. "Hmmm. It's kind of far east. Maybe we could . . ."

"Grab it!" Jill yelled. "You'll love it," she said to Martha.

Martha can be surprisingly indecisive, something we argue about constantly. If she is listening to the GPS and the voice says, "Turn left," she will wonder if the voice means *this* left, or maybe the *next* left. To me it's obvious. You say turn left; I turn left. I could not wrap my mind around the indecisiveness. She could not wrap her mind around why I'd get so annoyed.

Martha at work is an entirely different matter. She is steady and strong and opinionated. I love seeing her as a stage manager. I don't know what to say except this: She's super sexy. Truth. I wanted her trip planning to feel more like she was stage managing.

Suddenly Matt held his phone high in the air. "I got through!" Jill ran over and grabbed the phone, working the telephone rep for information.

"Nothing in the Big Sur area at all? Anything in Big Basin?"

A spot opened up on my computer. "Patrick's Point?" No one had heard of it. I booked two nights. It was three weeks in the future, and I didn't even know if we'd be in California then, but the pictures of the park were pretty.

"Henry Cowell!" Jill exclaimed. "We'll take it!"

By the end we had a hodgepodge of campsites, and very few were consecutive. Jill started to fill in the gaps. "OK. You'll drive to Linda and Paul's on Sunday and stay in their driveway for two nights. Then you'll head up the Pacific Coast Highway and go to Henry Cowell . . ." I couldn't keep up, but I was trying, peppering

Jill with questions as we looked at a state map. I really didn't know California well enough to make this kind of a plan, and Martha wasn't chiming in. I looked over at her and saw her lips pursing. I knew this look. She was about to cry.

Martha cries when she is overwhelmed. I assumed Jill knew this and had seen it, being her best friend and all. She hadn't. She looked at Martha as the tears fell, perplexed. "What is happening right now?"

Martha tried to explain that it was all moving too fast, and she wasn't sure how it would all work. Matt walked over and kissed Martha on the head, saying, "I feel this way all the time." He looked back at us, coffee in hand. "I've got to get to work. Good luck, you guys. It'll be fantastic. You have each other."

Jill and Martha talked, trying to work through why Martha was so overwhelmed, which overwhelmed Martha more. She left to get some air and I tried to explain it to Jill. "I dragged her out of New York, we spent three months in Cincinnati with both kids and my family, she had to work the entire trip across the country, Dot died, and, you know, what she hates more than anything is to make plans. She overloads."

Jill got it. "This is a lot of decisions at once."

"And you and I work fast."

Jill agreed. "I plan everything. All Matt has to do is get in the car."

"Right, and Martha likes it when I plan, but she wants to be involved. It's so annoying, she has these things called opinions." We laughed. It was nice to bond with Jill.

She grabbed some masks she'd made. "I made these for you guys, for the road." I looked at the huge pile next to her sewing machine, impressed. She explained, "I needed a project. I couldn't just sit around." I understood on a deep level.

We pulled out the next morning, our schedule mostly planned, but lots of room for Martha's opinions. I tried to schedule a healthy balance of seeing people (for her) and seeing things (for me).

◆ ◆ ◆

We spent over a month in California. We visited every corner, and while there were many takeaways, the single most surprising thing about California was the sheer number of pine trees.

Pine trees are everywhere. In all shapes and sizes, and they all smell delicious.

I grew up in a house that had a pine grove on the property. My Dad strung a hammock in between two of them, the sticky sap oozing onto the rope, the spiny needles landing like crosshairs on the holes of the braiding. I was a lonely kid, comforted by books and my dogs, so I would often pack up a sandwich, grab whichever *Little House on the Prairie* book I was rereading at the moment, grab my St. Bernard Patrick, and spend the day in the hammock. I'd close my eyes and swing, dreaming of the happy life I wanted as an adult, full of friends and Broadway, and breathe in the deep smell of the warm pine trees that surrounded me. Dappled by sunlight, these are some of the happiest moments of my childhood. Toward the end of college, I worked in Maine for several summers, not on the famous coastline, but interior Maine, where there are forests of pine trees. The resort where I worked had a curated pine path, a carpet of golden needles that led to the Music Hall, where I performed nightly. The scent of the pine trees and lake mixed with the smell of the dusty wood of the old Music Hall should be combined into a candle scent which I would call "Sharon Wheatley's Nostalgia."

California smelled the same way. It was delicious. Top to bottom, coast to inland, it's full of pines. We crisscrossed the state, visiting parks, camping in the pitch black. Sequoia and Kings Canyon national parks, Yosemite, Monterey, Big Sur, Patrick's Point. We took the Roaring Camp Railroad near the pines of Henry Cowell Redwoods State Park, riding through forests of pine trees so tall there was no sky to see. It was a healing time for us. While Martha had the stress of *Diana* behind her, I was still haunted by the loss of our jobs and the growing sense that it could be a long time before we returned to work. I closed my eyes, breathed deeply, reminding myself of when I was a young and lonely kid, swinging among the pine trees, with only my ambition to keep me company. My mantra then worked just as well now: *This is just a moment in time. You'll be OK. You'll be OK. You'll be OK.*

◆ ◆ ◆

Martha was confident and opinionated about everything in California once we left Jill's, from which place had the best Mexican food (Del Taco for fast food, Los Jarritos as a sit-down restaurant) to which highway to take at what time of day, no GPS needed (the 5 is packed, we're taking the 110). She regaled me with stories about her college survival jobs (Snappy Car Rental, the cafeteria of Harvey Mudd College). She slowed down and pointed at things with her arm out the window. "That's where my buddy Alan lived. We did a lot of coke. I was so skinny." I never did coke, I worked at my dad's tanning salon in college, and I ate burgers and fries. I was squarely Ohio. I loved California already, but seeing California through Martha's eyes was intoxicating.

We stayed in more driveways. Matt and Jill had friends whom we also knew, Linda and Paul, and they lived on a horse farm outside of San Luis Obispo. I wanted to go to San Luis Obispo, which people call SLO, because I had a friend there who is an eye doctor, and I wanted him to look at my tear duct which had been clogged and untreated for a year. I figured now was as good a time as any to deal with it. What else did I have to do? Let's have eye surgery! I called Larry, made an appointment, and then Martha called Linda and Paul to see if we could sleep in their driveway. As if sleeping in people's driveways was a normal thing we did every day.

Jill had already assessed Linda and Paul's driveway situation.

"Totally flat! No problem!"

It was true. It only took one leveler.

Linda and Paul's place was also epic, this time in beautiful California farm country.

They and their two kids were eating dinner out back when we arrived, in the dark, and we said our distant hellos. I didn't know them as well as Martha did, but I'd met them. The last time I'd seen them was backstage at *Come From Away* and I looked nothing like that person anymore. My hair was in ponytails, I had on no makeup, and I was tan. The actress version of me had never seemed further away.

Again, we dragged an extension cord to Linda and Paul's house and plugged in. I'd taken the time in LA to decorate in earnest, desperate to make the RV feel like home. I'd hung a string of lights from the front to the back of the RV, and now all that work was paying off, giving us some very cozy nighttime lighting.

In the morning we unplugged and drove down to SLO for my eye appointment. I'd worn glittery eyeliner for a press event, back in the days when I wore makeup and did press events, and the glitter had lodged in my tear duct, causing endless tears down the right side of my face. My eye had been swollen and tearing for so long that Melissa, the head of the wardrobe department of *Come From Away*, had provided a handkerchief for me so I could wipe my eye mid-show. I sent a text on the cast text thread. *You guys. I am finally getting my eye looked at.* Joel wrote back, *That's too bad. I will miss you crying at my excellent acting.*

Larry, my eye guy, had become my friend because he'd written me a fan letter. He read my first book and then his son Bryan had read it, and one thing led to another and now we were all friends. His wife Laurie invited me to dinner after my eye appointment with an added bonus of Bryan being in town, too. Larry took a look at my eye, deemed me as needing surgery, and tried to flush it out as best he could. I would have stayed in SLO and had surgery then and there, but the Covid-19 protocols were prohibitive. Instead, I had eye drops and dinner.

Bryan was a kid when I met him, but was now a casting director in LA. He and his family, like everyone, were starved to see new people, so we hung out in their backyard, drank wine from their vineyard, and talked show biz. Sparky, our attention-seeking Schnoodle and lone man on the trip, got a lot of attention from Laurie. She fed him s'mores all night, a taste he remembered for the rest of the trip, begging every time we made s'mores, which, if you are in an RV and cooking dinner over a campfire, is often.

We drove on and wrapped up our quartet of California driveway visits with the Dinaburgs in Sonoma. Dan and Jean were friends of mine from Quisisana, the previously mentioned piney resort in Maine where I'd worked and visited for years. The owner, our friend Jane Orans, died right before Covid-19 hit, and it was a huge loss to all of us who loved her. Martha and I had become increasingly close to Jean and Dan over the years. They visited us often, and despite numerous invitations to their Sonoma home, we never thought we'd make it out to them due to our work schedules. They had a flat driveway and were thrilled at the prospect of seeing us, so we headed off in their direction, taking the giant rig on the famous Pacific Coast Highway through Big Sur. Bonus points to Martha Donaldson, who drove that winding coast road like a boss. If this were a travel guide, I'd tell you to add the PCH[8] to your bucket list because while you've maybe seen it on every car commercial, you can't really get a real understanding of its beauty until you see it in person. And maybe take Martha as your driver.

Despite all this frivolity, Martha and I were arguing again because guess who was back in the RV with us? *Diana*. Not rehearsals, just more meetings and more emails about meetings and then more emails about emails about meetings. It wasn't as much as it had been on the first part of the trip, but it was enough for us to bicker and pick at each other.

Moments before we arrived at Jean and Dan's, we did that thing where you say, "Don't make me pull this RV over!" And then we actually did it. We pulled the RV over to argue something out.

I can't even remember what it was, but I can imagine I probably said something like *I'm going to get out and walk home because the whole trip is becoming one giant Zoom call with* Diana. And Martha probably said *No, you're not leaving, I'm leaving*.

And then probably Sparky barked at an anthill, and we laughed and got back in the RV and drove to Jean and Dan's house. You get the picture.

Jean had some health concerns that made Covid-19 a real threat, so we were extremely cautious as we visited them. We leveled and plugged in, then joined them for dinner, sitting outside and at the far end of a long table.

---

8   PCH = Pacific Coast Highway. That's some groovy California slang for all you non-Californians out there.

Jean instantly knew something was wrong, even at a distance.

"It's a lot of together time in that van, am I right, Broadway Babes?" Jean was a semi-retired therapist who had often listened—as a friend—to me and Martha as we sorted through various states of our relationship.

"I am requesting time alone with both of you."

Then she looked at Dan and said, "You're not invited, but I will fill you in since you always want to know what's going on."

"Whatever you say, Jean Star."

Dan was a fully retired psychiatrist and was, as Martha described him, "Adorable." He and Jean had practices in San Francisco and deeply loved the Bay Area. Dan wore striped socks with little German clogs while Jean wore shades of blue and artful jewelry. They dealt with retirement differently. Jean mentored kids in town, learned the mandolin, and wrote poetry. Dan played tennis, golf, and chess. They were a hoot and always had something going on.

"Did I tell you guys about our new sleep routine?" Jean asked. "You have to try it."

Dan interrupted Jean, causing her to give him the side-eye. "We read a whole study about sleeping with your mouth open and how bad it is for your health."

He leaned forward in his seat. "It can cause early dementia!"

Jean made a nonchalant face and looked at us. "You two are much younger than us so you don't have to worry about such things."

"Jeanie, it's never too early to think about your health."

They went back and forth for a minute—honestly it was nice to see two happily married people bickering—but we eventually got the whole story about the science of why a person needs to sleep with their mouth closed.

The story culminated with Jean saying, "So, here's the kicker. We tape our mouths shut when we go to bed!"

Martha shook her head in disbelief. "Wait. You what? You tape your mouths shut?"

"Yes! And we wear masks over our eyes!" Jean added.

"If you came into our bedroom, you'd think we'd been robbed," Dan told us matter-of-factly.

"Or dead," Jean suggested.

As we sat and laughed and drank local wine, I looked at Jean and Dan's gorgeous property. Here we were, deep in the wine country of California, and not doing the five-show weekend we were contracted to do. How would we ever be able to recover financially from the ruin of this virus? I had waited my whole life to finally have a job and it had evaporated. How would I ever provide even a fraction of the stability the Dinaburgs had?

I talked to Jean about it the next day in the two chairs she'd set up for this purpose, six feet apart in the front yard.

"We were scheduled to turn in the RV tomorrow, but we ended up extending it. They pushed back the date for Broadway reopening again."

"I saw that. September?"

"No. It was just announced. No theater through the end of 2020."

We talked about the devastation of that, my constant financial analysis and planning, and the difference between me and Martha.

"She seems totally fine without working. She's happy. I wish I could feel like that. Instead, I feel like the rug's been pulled out from under me. And now we're out in this RV—I don't even know who I am anymore. I wish I had Martha's, I don't know, ability to relax and enjoy."

Jean nodded in that therapist way. I kept talking.

"And then when she complains about having to work, I get so mad. I'm totally unreasonable."

Jean understood. "It's not unreasonable, you love your job. It makes sense, you waited a long time for it. And now the kids aren't here either, so no wonder you feel out of it. It's just you and the road in your gas-guzzling monstrosity."

Jean asked, "So is Martha's job done?"

"It keeps popping back up. The reason we were so late yesterday is because we had to find a place in the middle of nowhere on our way across the state from Yosemite. She had a meeting with the director and everyone about a possible recording."

We'd recently heard there were plans in place to record the cast album of *Diana* at some point in August. We didn't believe it. Everyone was still talking about the choral group in Washington State that had held a rehearsal during which one singer infected 87% of the choir. Many of them were quite sick and hospitalized and two of them died. Singing indoors became the poster child of the fastest way to spread Covid-19.

Jean wondered aloud, "So how do you make plans without knowing if she has to go back?"

"We just keep going, I guess. I have a zero-percent credit card and, as of now, the plan is to stay out until we pick up the kids at the end of the summer. I mean, we're this far in, why not keep going?"

Jean smiled. "It's smart. You're having your retirement now."

"Something like that. Once we go back to work, that's it. I'm working for as long as I humanly can."

"I'm glad we got you when we could, then." She smiled. "You've got a lot of pluck, my dear. Try to enjoy it."

Swimming in their pool surrounded by lavender and having dinners under the California stars certainly helped me forget, at least temporarily, that I'd rather be in my theater in Midtown Manhattan. We extended our trip and stayed for five lovely nights. I couldn't get the Joni Mitchell song out of my head, *Oh California . . ..will you take me as I am?*

We had our final stop in Northern California before heading up to Seattle, staying at a small state park called Patrick's Point. Again, I'm not a travel reviewer and this is not a travel guide, but I must tell you: the park sits on the Pacific coast where California borders Oregon and it is breathtaking. Two words: sea stacks. These mind-blowing stacks of rocks in the ocean—I didn't know they existed. If you get a chance, go see them. Strong, stand-alone formations in the powerful swirl of the surf.

I could relate.

CHAPTER 11

AFRICA, 1978

I remember picking my dad up at the airport, watching the baggage carousel with him in his khaki safari outfit, using my eagle eyes to spot any packages wrapped in foreign newspaper and plastic.

He assured me, "You can't miss them, honey. They're gigantic."

Sure enough, one of them was almost as tall as me, and I was pretty tall for an eleven-year-old. I couldn't wait to see what was inside it, but my eye was drawn to my dad, who was trying to embrace my mother as she waited, arms crossed, on the far end of baggage claim. I could see him flirting and cajoling with her, but she wasn't having it.

My father had gone to Africa. He'd watched animal shows his whole life, like it was his job, and had finally decided it was time for him to see these majestic animals for himself. It was 1978, and he booked a safari in Africa, telling my mom, "I'll have a layover in New York on the way and check on Susan at college. Two birds with one stone."

My mother raised her eyebrow and shook her head. I didn't know if it was because my sister went to school in New Haven, too far from Kennedy airport for a quick check-in, or if it was because we were broke and my mother didn't approve. Or all of the above.

He had gone despite her disapproval and now he was back, three weeks later, with foreign and oddly shaped packages. I was excited to see what was in them. My mother looked like she was contemplating boarding a plane in the opposite direction.

The car ride home was not silent, but it was one-sided. As my dad drove us, he regaled us with stories of what he'd seen. The Masai, the charging elephants. "The cape buffalo is the meanest animal in Africa, I'll bet you didn't know that, did you?" I didn't. I assumed it was a lion. "A lion won't eat you just to eat you, that's a polar bear. And a cape buffalo will kill you and leave you for dead. Then the vultures will take care of you."

I pictured myself as a picked-over skeleton on the brown grasses of Africa. My mom wasn't talking. I wondered if she was listening.

Then she spoke. "Charlie, we got the tax bill. I don't know how we are going to pay it. And Susan's tuition is due . . ." She started to cry.

"Don't you start doing that." He was furious. "Don't you ruin my first night home with money talk. I just landed after the trip of my life, and you are trying to bring me down."

I knew the tax bill was $23,000. And I knew Susan's tuition was $12,000. And I knew how much was in their bank account. Negative $132. My mom had fretted over the big blue checkbook, crying and telling me all about it.

My Dad had a solution. "We sold the boat. That will cover it."

I knew something else, too. My Dad had sold the boat for cash and stored the money in rolled-up bills in the safe upstairs under my mom's vanity in their bedroom. My mom told me the combination, 6-64-32, and all the turns. Three times right, once left all the way around, and then a half turn to the right. I'd been in the safe a lot. I knew better than to say anything, but in the car home from the airport I did suddenly have a big stomachache. I wondered if my mom did, too.

When we got home, my dad insisted on a big show-and-tell, unwrapping the packages one by one, revealing giant carvings of elephants and giraffes. He looked at my mom and said, "I got the giraffes for you, honey. I know they are your favorite." She only half smiled, but it was something. He pulled out a long tail with a wooden and leather handle and handed it to me. "Do you know what this is?" He didn't wait for a response. "It's a fly whisk. That's a horse tail on there, and you swipe it around to keep the bugs away." I told him I loved it, but I was also kind of grossed out. I was hoping he'd bring me a doll, like my mom did when she traveled. But I also knew he shouldn't have bought anything, so I felt guilty for even thinking that.

As he started to tell stories of hippos at the watering hole and litters of cheetahs, my mom cut him off. "Charlie, it's late. I have to work in the morning and Sharon has school."

"I'm okay!" I said.

"To bed," she said.

As I made my way up the stairs, I heard them start to argue, my dad mad and disappointed. "You've been a bummer all night! Why are you bringing me down like this?"

"How are we going to pay for all this? What am I supposed to tell the IRS? My husband went on safari and blew all our money?"

My dad lost it. "I *told* you. We have the boat money." My mom started to cry. I hustled up the steps and dove into bed, covering my ears.

We'd spent the boat money. Not all at once, but in small shopping sprees, buying me some winter clothes, my mom a new coat, my brother a new transmission for his car. The money was nearly gone, the tube of cash rolled up in the rubber band smaller and smaller every time my mother sent me up for more.

"Go get some more boat money, Sharon."

"Okay!" I'd say.

It was fun in the moment. Like we were doing something bad. Like when I snuck nacho cheese Doritos. I liked being in this heist with my mom. I'd even started sleeping with her while my dad was gone, snuggling up to her as she talked about how ridiculous and irresponsible he was. His side of the bed smelled, but I took fragrant bubble baths before bed and had sprayed some of my mom's Estee Lauder perfume on the sheets, so it was smelling better. My own bed felt foreign and cold as I listened to them argue. I worried about being an accomplice to the crime. Batman and Robin gone bad.

When my mom finally came clean about the boat, days later, my dad laughed until he cried. "So, are you telling me you spent that money $20 at a time?"

She sobbed. "Yes."

"Well, did you enjoy yourself?"

She answered meekly. "Kind of. If I didn't think about it too much."

"That's all I care about, kid. I'll make the money back. Don't you worry about it. Is there any money left?" She was silent.

"There's $925 left," I yelled. I'd been sitting on my usual eaves-dropping spot at the top of the stairs.

My Dad laughed heartily. "Well then, Sharon, go get it and let's take your mother out and buy her something nice with it." I ran to the safe just as I heard him say, "Maybe a nice opal bracelet to go with your ring?"

"Charlie, NO."

I wondered if maybe I could get a little something since all I had was a stupid horse tail.

"All I have to do is sell one pool to pay for all of this." He always said this.

"Your math is wrong and it's November. No one is buying a pool in November."

"Don't bring me down!" was the last thing I heard as I headed back to my mom's vanity.

◆ ◆ ◆

A few weeks later we had "Career Day" in my class and a bunch of parents came to talk about what they did for a living. A doctor. A scientist. A paralegal. My dad came to my class, dressed in his head-to-toe safari outfit, and told the students, "My name is Charles Wheatley, and I am an African wildlife expert. I go on adventures for a living." The kids all ooooed and aahed over his pictures of hyenas tearing apart carcasses.

He gave me a wink as he walked out. "Pretty good, huh, kid?"

Later, Joe Mitchell, the cutest kid in my class, told me my dad was cool and we must be rich.

I didn't know what to say. I wanted to tell him my dad built swimming pools and we didn't have the money for the taxes. But that seemed boring, so I didn't say anything at all. I let him think what he wanted.

But I still knew.

My mom did, too. She sold the opals and scheduled a payment plan with the IRS. My dad was mad about it, but I wasn't.

I was relieved.

CHAPTER 12

THE NORTHWEST

Coming into Seattle, I was struck by a crazy idea. I looked up my friend Elisabeth, the producing director of the Seattle Repertory Theatre, and sent her a message.

YOU SENT JULY 15, 2020

Elisabeth! Hello there.

I was trying to find an email or phone number for you, but all I seem to have is Facebook!

Martha and I are heading into Seattle tomorrow, and we wondered if we could park on any level section of the Seattle Rep property for a night? That would be Thursday night.

Maybe? Possible?

I hope you and your family are great!!! WE MISS THEATER. Hang in there.

ELISABETH SENT JULY 15, 2020

What kind of vehicle do you have? What time would you arrive?

YOU SENT JULY 15, 2020

We have a thirty-foot Cruise America RV. Only one night. Coming from Eugene, Oregon so maybe 4 or 5?

ELISABETH SENT JULY 15, 2020

Let me check with operations!

Also - the angle off the street is pretty tight. 53' semis can back in (which you'd have to do), but it's a tight squeeze.

Parking in the loading dock of a theater? This had to rank as the oddest thing we'd done, and it wasn't easy. The angle off Mercer Street into the lot was pretty tight, and I ended up stopping traffic on 2nd and directing Martha as she backed in. She nailed it and managed to avoid big concrete blocks and a low-hanging awning, so we pretty much felt like bad asses.

Before *Come From Away* was on Broadway, we played several cities out of town, including a sold-out run at the Seattle Repertory Theatre. It was a magical time for all of us involved in the show, back when we were still wondering how far the show might go. Martha and I had met during the La Jolla Playhouse run of the show, but she'd left to do another Broadway show. Despite that, she'd flown to see me in Seattle many times, and we counted our time during the Seattle Rep run as some of the most romantic and critical times of our relationship. We decided to call Kendra and Chad, friends of ours, original cast members of *Come From Away*, and current residents of Seattle, to see if they wanted to come down and visit us. In the parking lot. Of the theater. Because that's what 2020 had brought us to. Chad was unavailable but Kendra joined us, laughing as she approached the RV.

"I don't know if you guys are geniuses or crazy, but I sure am glad to see you! Can we hug? I never know what to do."

We compromised; we hugged but held our breath. She held out a gift bag. What do you bring to people living in an RV? She brought a bottle of wine and a candle. Emily Post, take note.

We had a terrific night locked into the loading dock, laughing, crying, and catching up. We took pictures and sent them to the whole *Come From Away* cast. After Kendra left, we went into the dark and empty theater building. It marked the first time since our shows stopped that we'd been in a theater, and we could see that Seattle Rep had shut down quickly as well; the set for their production of August Wilson's *Jitney* was still on the stage, frozen in time. We walked around the empty halls and through the scene shop, basking in the familiar combination of smells; the makeup and hairspray near the dressing rooms, the paint and fresh-cut wood smell from the vast scene shop, and the slightest hint of spilled wine still lingering in the lobby. The name of this candle scent would be "Smell of the Greasepaint, Roar of the Crowd." Martha had brought the Flame Thrower, and we used it as a spotlight to illuminate the stage from the house seats, commenting on how both creepy and awesome it all was. And sad. I had a lot of trouble sleeping that night. It felt like everything I'd tried to push away by going on a remote RV trip had found me, reminding me I was desperate for the world to restart.

The next morning, we were set to move to the driveway of my cousins, Becky and Kim, both doctors who lived in Seattle. We were trying to make the bed.

"Ethel, move." Martha nudged Ethel off the bed. But Ethel wouldn't move.

"I'll get her." I went over and picked up Ethel, who had been historically plump from birth, egged on by my mom and dad, who had kept a cereal bowl full of food for her on top of their dryer. You could hear Ethel land on the dryer from most places in my parents' house. When my mom died and my dad was moved to a memory care unit that did not allow pets, Ethel had landed with the cat-whisperer, Martha. She'd been an inside/outside cat with my parents and had become so nimble in her RV escapes that we'd finally bought her a leash and harness. When we parked the RV at camp, we'd tie Ethel up to the back bumper and allow her to wander around while we made dinner.

It became a joke between us.

Did you remember to unleash Ethel?

I scooped Ethel up and put her down in the kitchen. She promptly fell over.

Martha saw it. "Uh-oh. That's not good." She grabbed her and took her outside, setting her down on the asphalt of the parking lot. "Maybe she just needs some room." Ethel fell over again, and then curled into a ball like a pill bug.

I immediately started to cry like a small child. "Martha! She can't die!" I sat down on the steps of the RV, surprised by the strength of my own emotion. It wasn't like I was so attached to Ethel exactly, but I was extremely invested in what Ethel meant to my parents, and my connection to them through her. Every time I petted her, I could picture my mom snuggling with her, or my dad saying *Get off me, cat!* when Ethel would jump up and invade his newspaper reading. They were a threesome, and she was the final holdout.

Martha, having just experienced the death of a pet of her own, understood. "We'll get her to the vet." She scooped her up and placed her in my arms, gathered the last of our goods, and ushered us all back into the RV. She got into the driver's seat and handed me her phone, the GPS set for a nearby animal hospital.

I looked at Martha and said, "We can't have the story be that two cats died on this trip. We'll look like cat-killers."

"Agreed." She drove faster.

Seattle is full of steep, narrow streets, and Martha navigated them as if we were in a Mini, not a thirty-foot-long pet infirmary. She pulled up outside the hospital and called in. They told us, once again, to bring her to the door and not to come in. We were becoming pros at this. I looked at Martha, "When was Dot's ship set to sail? Maybe we can get Ethel on board, too." Then I cried harder.

Martha laughed gently and said, "I don't think we're there yet." She took her to the door and dropped her off. "They said they'll call when they know more." She looked at her watch. "The wedding starts in thirty minutes."

"Oh my God, I forgot." Two friends of ours, Ellen and Georgia, who'd met at our wedding, were getting married that afternoon and live-streaming the event on Zoom. I looked around. "Maybe we can just park somewhere and watch it while we wait to hear about Ethel?"

We snaked around the streets and finally, with time running out, settled on a small alley by a parking lot. It wasn't ideal but it would have to do, and hopefully getting towed would not be added to our day's activities. As we prepared to log on to the wedding on Martha's phone, we laughed. "What do we wear to a Zoom wedding?" We quickly changed our shirts, I put in earrings and Martha put product in her hair, and we watched our friends wed.

Almost immediately after the vows, the phone rang, and it was the vet. Ethel had suffered a "neurological episode." They'd run some tests and wanted to do an MRI on her for further information, and when I asked how much this might cost, the bill was in the thousands. I asked if they could hold on a minute and put the phone on mute. I looked at Martha.

"How deep are we going to go into this?" I was a little panicky. "I am afraid of getting into MRIs and further testing for a kitty who is seventeen. Does that make me heartless?" But before she could answer, I already knew. Just before the pandemic we'd had her in for a surgery that was supposed to help her with congestion. At the end of the day the surgery had cost almost $2,000, and, as it turned out, she was still congested. Susan and Buzz had weighed in at the time, saying we should not spend a fortune on Ethel.

Susan was pragmatic. "She's old. Mom and Dad would not want you to go broke paying for that cat." Now, swerving through Seattle, I didn't bother to text them for advice, I knew what they would say.

"My parents would not want this," I told Martha. "No way. We've done great by her."

Martha was thoughtful. "I agree with you." Martha was the one who would spend endless amounts of money on any animal, so if she agreed, I knew I was morally in the clear. I got back on the phone.

"How much would it cost me to come and pick her up right now?"

$1100 later, I had Ethel in a cardboard box and we were heading out to Becky and Kim's.

Becky, my first cousin on my dad's side, and her husband, Kim, have been together since I was a kid, so I'm equally close to both of them. Becky is interested in long dinners and conversations while Kim is an avid outdoorsman. As I held the box I told Martha, "It feels right for Ethel to die at Becky and Kim's. They loved my mom and dad." Martha nodded as she drove. I went on. "In fact, they loved Becky and Kim's house. They would fully support Ethel being buried in their yard. Kim is an animal guy, like my dad was. He'll take care of everything. He's like that." As sad as I was, I could see the events play out in my head and I felt at peace. "We'll make Ethel as comfortable as possible and wait for the end." I had opted to get the painkillers from the vet. They said they were essential. Poor Ethel was dopey, but she seemed peaceful.

We arrived at Becky and Kim's beautiful and pine-tree-filled neighborhood due east of downtown, then performed the usual leveling and plugging in of our trusty extension cord. They greeted us heartily, and listened clinically, as doctors, to Ethel's prognosis, Becky assuring me their family had buried many beloved family pets in their yard.

"If it's Ethel's time, she'll be in good company." As it turns out, Kim was also an assistant to a vet in his youth, so he took an interest in Ethel immediately.

"Put her down and let me see her walk around." He watched as Ethel dragged herself by her front legs, seal-style.

"I was telling Martha all about your relationship with my parents and how apt it seemed should Ethel die while we are here." I was trying to hold in the ugly-cry I felt looming.

Kim gently set Ethel back up on all four legs and gave her a quick exam. She flopped over again.

"They gave you painkillers?"

"Yes, they insisted." I told him the name and he shook his head.

"That's some strong shit. I don't think she needs it. Let's see how she does once these opioids are out of her system."

They built a giant fire in their yard, and we spent several nights there, talking about everything and everyone—their kids, Tobi and Charlotte, and the extended family. We left Ethel in the RV with the door open and one morning as we talked and had coffee, we heard a sliding sound with a slightly disconcerting thump, only to see that Ethel had dragged herself to the door and down the stairs. She lay on the grass and looked around. I went to scoop her up, but Kim stopped me.

"She seems interested in her surroundings, that's always a good sign. People recover from strokes, and so do cats."

Slowly she started reusing her back legs, limping, but more mobile. She started to get far enough away that Sparky, who was leashed to the RV, would whimper, wanting his freedom, too. She started to roam their large yard, getting lost, with Becky calling, "Ethel's over here!" or Kim finding her at the front door of their house. One day we totally lost her until Martha walked the neighborhood, finding her several houses down.

Kim gave her a rough pat on the head, saying, "Good for you, Ethel. You've got some kick in you yet. Charlie and Mary Jo would be proud." He said to us, "It's time for you to start leashing her up again so she isn't snatched by a wild critter round these parts."

He wasn't kidding. The next morning there was bear poop next to the RV. Ethel, meanwhile, had made it back up on our bed and walked all over us for petting, proving she was becoming nimbler and her normal self.

◆ ◆ ◆

Despite growing up in Cincinnati, Becky and Kim knew the Northwest like the back of their hand. They'd taken their kids backpacking, fly-fishing, and camping all through the area, so when we told them our idea to head to the Olympic Peninsula, and then over to Yellowstone, they had enthusiastic recommendations. *Take the ferry. Eat pizza at Waterfront Pizza. Make sure you hike up and see the harrier hawks hunt and hang out in the wind. Head out to La Push.* We knew we were getting expert and excellent advice, and after departing their lovely and mostly level driveway we drove that giant RV onto a ferry bound for the OP (local speak for Olympic Peninsula). We parked the RV alongside tractor trailers and Martha, always worried about weight, was gobsmacked. "How does this thing not sink? MIRACULOUS."

After a gorgeous day of pizza and biking in and around Port Townsend, Martha and I headed to our RV park in Sequim, a town famous for lavender. We were en route and, as always, racing against the sun, which was setting in a spectacular display, when Martha took a wrong turn.

"Oh crap. Now what have I done." The GPS started swirling, looking for another route. Martha slowed down. "I'll just pull in here and turn around." She pulled onto a beautiful gravel driveway, surrounded by pine trees and tall, waving grasses—a golf course. At the end there was a small parking lot which had an entrance and exit at both ends. "Oh good. I don't even have to back up." Martha had become good at wielding the RV, always joking that she forgot how big it was until she got out and looked at it from the outside. She turned the corner with gusto, when suddenly there was the hideous noise of shredding metal, followed by a loud boom.

"Martha! Stop! Stop!" I jumped out and looked in the back, praying I'd see nothing.

Hidden in the tall grasses was a fire hydrant. We'd clipped it and its revenge was to shred the side of the RV and tire, all the way down to the tire's metal rim.

"Oh God, oh no!" Martha had jumped out of the RV to see the damage. Sparky stuck his nose out the screen, whimpering to get out. "We are so screwed."

I immediately thought of George. He'd told us to text him with any issues, and he'd encouraged us to get the bumper-to-bumper additional insurance coverage, which, thank God, we'd done. "We'll be ok," I assured Martha. "The insurance will cover this." Martha seemed less sure.

"Look around. We are in the middle of nowhere and the sun is setting. It'll be pitch black in minutes. We can't drive like this." Here we were in the middle of vampire country (the *Twilight* series was set nearby), with nothing. And then my dad's voice rang in my head, *This is an adventure, kid. Enjoy it!* I felt a great sense of calm and a twinge of giddiness. I shared it with Mar.

"Honey. We are in a fully stocked RV with a generator. Even if we have to stay here all night, it's barely different than if we'd made it to the RV park. And I seriously doubt the park would have a better view than this." The sky was variations of a darkening blue, shot through with vivid pink and orange as the sun set. We were surrounded by tall pines and birds soaring overhead, and the expansive green golf course. "If my dad were here, he'd tell us to go play golf."

She laughed. "Too bad we don't have any clubs. We have just about everything else."

More than you know, I thought.

I opened the garage door, which had not been destroyed by the fire hydrant, and pulled out my cozy high-backed chair, getting to work on my phone.

"Honey, I'll call Cruise America, and you text George. If we can't get anyone out here, we'll grill up the turkey burgers." Martha agreed.

Turns out, there was a guy with a truck nearby, and he got to us within minutes. We were shocked. Martha joked, "We could break down on the FDR in the middle of Manhattan and not get service like this." Meanwhile, George had returned Martha's call and she came back with some news. "George says we have to empty out the basement to get to the spare."

Uh-oh. Lucy had a lot in that basement that Desi didn't know about.

I answered her, trying to appear calm. "I think you mean garage." I got to work. "I'll take care of it. You relax." Maybe I could hide it. If a fire hydrant could disappear in that grass, I mused, anything could.

Of course, it became a huge task, taking off the bikes and the bike rack and then emptying out every single thing. Eugene-the-tire-guy, a local guy with a tow truck, showed up, and pretty soon it was all three of us, pulling out boxes of *Toy Story* toys, American Girl Doll furniture, original paintings, and a mirror.

"A mirror???" Martha exclaimed. I just shrugged. It was a great mirror. Mid-century modern and awesome. I had to have it. We leaned it all against a rustic wooden fence next to the seventeenth hole.

An hour later we were all packed up to go, spare tire on, just as twilight took over. Eugene-the-tire-guy, a Coronavirus non-believer, sent us off into the night with some final reminders. "You'll need to get that tire fixed immediately. Go to Port Angeles, they'll have what you need. And those masks are a ridiculous waste of money."

We waved goodbye, thanked him for saving us, and got back on the road.

◆ ◆ ◆

The Olympic Peninsula is spectacular. Probably #1 on my list of places I'd want to return to. Martha and I laughed and soaked it all in, the deep green of the pine trees like a bath for our eyes. We extended our trip, and I could feel something starting to unwind. Finally.

After camping in some weather uncharacteristic for the Olympic Peninsula—sunny during the day, and dry but crisp at night—we headed to our next big stop: Yellowstone. On the way we stopped by Bellingham, Washington, where Ian, a dear friend of ours, and his son Charlie were staying in a family home. Ian is the music supervisor for both *Come From Away* and *Diana*, and he's always up on all the latest info, which we were dying to hear. We pulled into the driveway, which was directly across from a gorgeous lake, but also so close to the road that the RV shook every time someone drove by. We started pummeling him with questions before we even leveled.

"What have you heard about *Diana*?" Martha wanted to get right to it. "Are we really recording a cast album?"

"Oh, totally, and that's not all of it. Have you not heard?"

"No! Tell me!"

Poor Charlie, who was eight, had lost his fun, big sister to a weekend camping trip, and now was stuck with all the constant grownup talk.

"Dad!" Ian looked over and waved a pouting Charlie to his side.

"I promised Charlie I'd jump in the lake with him. Do you want to come?" He laughed as our faces fell, wanting information first. "It's a cliff-hanger! I'll fill you in as we swim." Mar and I jumped in our suits and joined them on the dock. Martha and Ian paired off, while I threw rafts and floaty toys at Charlie to make him laugh. All I wanted was to hear what Martha and Ian were saying, but since I'd assumed the Mary Poppins role with Charlie, I got my info in snippets, learning there was going to be a film made of *Diana* for Netflix. I had a million questions and no time to ask them. I got some time with Ian later, as we built the fire for dinner.

"Is this really going to happen, Ian? When?"

"Soon. Really soon. The cast album recording will be in New Jersey, and then we will move into New York City to rehearse and shoot the show as a film for Netflix. Massive Covid-19 protocols. I'm planning to fly back to New Jersey to start my two-week quarantine this weekend."

"This weekend?" I looked around at where we were, literally on the other side of the country. "It's such a roller coaster, Ian. We just found out Broadway wasn't coming back until January at the earliest. We thought we were in the clear to stay out."

We'd just called George and extended the rental to the end of the summer, committing to picking up Tobi and Charlotte in the RV. Why have everyone get on a plane if we could avoid it? What else did we have to do? It also meant Charlotte would get a crack at all the RV fun after hearing about it from all of us.

Ian gestured at the RV. "What are you guys going to do?"

I looked over at Martha, who was making fart noises with her hands while floating in a giant swan. "I don't know." As we ate dinner, I did the math. If they were going to start in three weeks, that meant we had a week to get Martha to New York or New Jersey to start her quarantine. One week.

We spent two nights at Ian's, hopeful he'd get more information before we left, but he didn't.

"Who knows? Maybe the whole thing will fall apart!" he said to Martha. "But if we do it, it's going to be really awesome. And great money."

Martha took an *I'll believe it when I see it* attitude, but she seemed distracted and distant. I wished they were filming *Come From Away* instead. I felt pouty. As we drove away from Ian's it felt like there'd been a barometric pressure change but we were ignoring it. Like trying to enjoy a picnic as you hear distant thunder.

We'd become increasingly good at contingency plans. If there was a Covid-19 outbreak in a certain part of the country, we maneuvered around it. If we struggled to find a campground, we'd rethink our plans and find a new, just as fun place to go that had availability. So when *Diana* started creeping back into the picture, we ran through every possibility under the sun. It became our whack-a-mole problem. We'd discuss it, we'd get frustrated, we'd decide to ignore it, and then it'd pop back up.

One day, as we walked Sparky around a brewery in Montana, Martha made a decision. "If I worry about this, we're going to ruin the good time we're having." I nodded my head in agreement. We both jumped in alarm when a giant sprinkler popped on right next to us, meant to hydrate the grass in an outdoor amphitheater next to the brewery. There was caution tape and signs saying *Concerts canceled for the season due to Covid-19.*

"Martha, if they can't even have a concert in a field in the middle of nowhere, Montana, how will they manage to pull off *Diana?*"

"Seriously! The whole show? At the theater? During Covid? It sounds like a nightmare of logistics."

"Don't worry about it. Besides," I added, "you won't have any cell service in Yellowstone, so they can't reach you even if they want to."

Yellowstone National Park seemed almost too on the nose to visit. Everyone goes to Yellowstone. Yawn. We weren't planning to go, choosing places off the beaten path instead, but Kim changed our mind about all of it. He'd been calling and texting as we crossed into Montana, doubling down on his own advice like he was afraid we'd ignore him.

"Yellowstone is too cool to miss and fewer tourists this year means more wildlife now." As a doctor he also kept us up to date on the latest Covid-19 hotspots, which were always changing. The virus had spread to the northern states, and he was concerned. "Avoid Idaho entirely. If you have to gas up, keep your mask on and keep going."

Kim became our go-to guide for this portion of the trip. He sent us texts like *Where are my Broadway Ladies? I want to steer you off the interstate for best drive to YNP.*[9]

I believe in taking advice from smart people, so we called him back, turned off our GPS, and went the Kim route, following his advice to the letter. He drove us along the backroad to Yellowstone,

---

9   YNP = Yellowstone National Park, mountain-man style.

I-287, which, dear reader, again, I am not a travel guide, but Kim is smart, and I am here to confirm that his routes were, as he described, "B-E-fuckin-utiful."

As we drove along beautiful I-287, we heard a strange noise. It sounded like someone was tossing small pebbles onto the roof of the RV. Martha and I were both freaked out until we figured out what it was.

We'd been on the road for forty-six days, and this was the first time it had rained.

Kim and Becky had enthusiastically talked about the calderas and rock formations and gone into great detail about the geysers, which, as we entered Yellowstone, were readily apparent and on display. I got a D in geology, so while it was all beautiful, it wasn't what I wanted to cash in my chips for. I had one goal.

Wildlife. And wow, did I get a ton of it. It. Was. Awesome. I will not go on and on about Yellowstone because there are books ad nauseam about it, so I will leave you with this. You should go. And I am not kidding around. And you should go in an RV and camp there because it's nice to always have a bathroom. And also bring binoculars. But call Kim first to get all the best science information, and then call me for campground and RV advice because I have gobs of opinions and we stayed in nearly every one of them.

◆ ◆ ◆

Coming out of Yellowstone still with no confirmed *Diana* news, we took another Kim and Becky special, a route called the Beartooth Highway. It was named the most beautiful road in America by Charles Kuralt, which might ring a bell for those readers over seventy. I shall give you the Beartooth Highway wrap-up. Really old rocks (ask Kim how old), beautiful views (ask Martha because my eyes were closed in terror), it will probably snow (it's only open in the summer due to the altitude), and there is a great ice cream place in a nearby town called Silverton. Call Becky and she'll tell you the name of the ice cream place. Maybe Wilcox? Also, call up Martha or Kim and see if they can be your drivers because friends, it's not for a wimp, and my knuckles are permanently white from hanging on.

And how it applies to this narrative is this: we took the Beartooth Highway to a laundry room.

◆ ◆ ◆

The funny thing about an RV is you always have everything with you. It really is like driving around with your whole house. Martha still managed to forget this, and we'd be driving down the road and she'd say, "I think I forgot my bathing suit!" and I'd just wait, knowing she'd get it, just to hear her laugh and say, "Oh *right*. It's all in here!"

And, just like in a house, we had chores to do. The biggest one being laundry.

Martha self-describes as being "controlling about laundry." I hate to do laundry, so in that way we are a perfect match. Every once in a while, as she sorts the laundry within an inch of its life, she'll look at me and say, "Are you sure it's okay that I always do the laundry?"

I don't even pretend to be anything but thrilled. I also know that doing laundry is how Martha resets. It's her Zen time: she has a task, she knows how to do it, and she knows when it's done. Many, many times I've watched Martha, upset over something, sling a laundry bag on her back and disappear, returning with neatly folded clothes and a fresh outlook. I figured *Diana* was heavy on her mind, and a few loads of laundry might make her feel better. Or at least more in control.

This RV campground in Hardin, Montana, was on the fancier side, which, in Martha language, means it had a nice laundry room.

After we'd pulled in and found our spot, Martha started to collect the laundry, which we kept in a combination of cardboard boxes we'd cut down to fit in the awkward RV cabinets. When Martha does laundry she washes everything, including the shirt off her back. She took piles of laundry while I started cleaning the floors, which were a piney, muddy mess from Yellowstone. Eventually she came back, remarkably un-Zen, as I was beating a rug outside.

"I have a phone meeting about *Diana* in ten minutes, so let's see what that brings." She stomped away. Instant stomachache.

What was meant to be a sleepy Sunday in Montana, spent regrouping and cleaning, had suddenly become our most stressful day yet. Charlotte sent a text and asked what we were up to. I wrote her back and said, "Worry cleaning."

I watched Martha talk on the phone and tried to discern what she was feeling. I saw a lot of laughing and note-taking, but that was par for the course. When she finally hung up and sat still, looking around at the sky, I sat in my chair and waited for her to come to me.

"August 13th is the day I report to start quarantine. It's all happening. The cast album and the Netflix movie. I won't be done until the end of September." I looked at her and waited to hear how she felt about it. I knew how I felt about it. I didn't want her to leave at all. But this was an awesome opportunity, and I did not want to spoil it. "It's incredible, right?" She looked at me, seemingly in shock. "I really did not believe for one second that they'd really pull this off. I cannot even imagine what all the Covid-19 protocols are going to be, and what that means for us. Wow! Seriously. Dude. This is huge!"

Despite what she said, I could feel a palpable change in Martha, like she'd left Montana and was already in the rehearsal room. Back in the RV, she picked up the laundry she'd been folding on the picnic table. "I need to make a calendar and think about what we're going to need in New Jersey . . ." Her voice trailed off as the door slammed behind her. Sparky followed her, as far as his leash would allow, whimpering at the door for her to come back.

I gave him a pat on the head as I walked to the door. "It's you and me now, buddy."

CHAPTER 13

THE TURNAROUND

"We have eight days to get you home," I said, the oversized Adventure Edition of the National Geographic Road Atlas, a legal pad, and a pen spread out in front of us. Martha had her phone with the calculator open.

We calculated every version of what to do. The most obvious and easiest choice was to turn left out of Montana and head southeast, returning me and the RV to Cincinnati. From there Martha could drive to New York City, avoiding an airplane and exposure to Covid-19. She loved this idea.

"You could come with me! And quarantine with me in the apartment!" Before I could respond she had another option.

"You could stay in Cincinnati! Have the kids meet you there! Then drive back to New York in time for school." I weighed that idea.

"Or," Martha said, "you could stay out and drive the kids back by yourself. But I'd have some serious FOMO." FOMO, or Fear Of Missing Out, was a big thing in Martha's life. She wanted to have fun in all the places all the time.

We went through options for hours, filling the legal pad with calculations of mileage and possible routes. One thing was certain. We had to get out of Montana, which was far from everywhere and, according to our mountain guide and medical doctor Kim, was a

Covid-19 hotspot. We packed up and drove south, back through Yellowstone, heading to Salt Lake City, which was at the crossroads of all options.

Mar hooked up to the Wi-Fi, fielded emails and phone calls, prepped her team, and started to make a calendar for the upcoming recording and filming. She knew what she had to do and where she had to be. I was the one that had to make decisions. I sat outside in the ugly cement RV park, surrounded by beautiful mountains, and thought it through. Making decisions on my own can be hard for me.

I used to live my life by committee, rarely making any decision alone, something that annoyed me—I wanted to learn to think for myself. The better part of twenty years in therapy was spent getting my parents out of my head, and now that they were both gone, I wanted nothing more than to call them up so they could tell me exactly what to do. Surely, I could conjure them. I wanted a crystal ball or a psychic or a Ouija board, but even without any of that, slowly, it came to me.

Mom would have told me to drive back to Cincinnati, turn in the RV, go back to New York with Martha, and have the kids fly directly to New York at the end of the summer. It was practical and financially responsible. She would have wrung her hands with worry over the money and my ability to drive the RV alone.

Dad would have told me to drive that RV to San Diego, let Martha go on to New York, and for me to stay out and have a great adventure with the kids. He would have mocked the concern that I was running out of money. Fun comes first. No fear. Don't doubt, drive.

But I did have fear. So *much* fear. Who was I without Martha? Could I drive it? Could I dump it? Could I cook it? Could I pay for it? My gut said no. I dug deeper. My gut could be an unreliable scaredy-cat.

A long time ago I wrote a book about becoming the person you *want* to be, which does not always line up with the person you *are* in that moment. When I was quiet with myself and really, really thought about it, the answer was clear. I *wanted* to drive to San Diego, drop Martha off at the airport, pick up the kids, and take them on an epic adventure. I had the time. I sort of had the money, and—despite my total anxiety at the thought of it—I had driven this route before.

Martha popped out of the RV with an energy only seen when prepping for filming a gigantic musical for Netflix.

"I'm kicking ass and taking names!" She did a small dance in front of me that included a lot of boxing moves and *pow pow* sounds. Sparky jumped off my gloomy lap, jumping up on Martha to join in the fun. After telling me all the things she was up to, she focused on me.

"So. What are you thinking? Are we Ohio bound or is it California here we come?"

My gut rang out: Don't doubt, drive.

"I want to go get the kids."

"That's my girl! You've got this!"

We made a plan, checked out of the KOA in Salt Lake, and headed to California. We had enough time to make a couple of stop-offs before Martha was done with her RV time, so I let her make the call. "I want to go see Jean and Dan again!"

We arrived in Sonoma and settled right back into our spot. Jean set up her lawn chair therapy office while Martha and Dan took our gray wastewater from the shower and sink and dumped it out bucket by bucket on the roots of their trees.

"I'll take any water I can get," Dan said. "It's fire season and dry as a bone." While Martha and Dan watered, Jean and I talked.

"So, girlfriend. You think you're ready to drive this Holiday Inn around by yourself?"

I started to cry.

I hadn't talked much about my driving anxiety. It was embarrassing. Martha had driven most of the trip, and she had for sure driven *all* the hard parts of the trip.

I've found, in my years of anxiety experience, that talking about anxiety begets more anxiety in me, so I'd held it in. The stupidest part is, I'm an excellent driver. My anxiety made absolutely no sense—absolutely zero sense. I had driven my entire life, proudly having a car always from the moment I'd turned sixteen. Even in Midtown Manhattan! For some people an inability to drive was an inconvenience. For me it felt like a disability.

I let it all out with Jean.

Pretty soon Dan and Martha got too curious to leave us alone, so they came over with their buckets and pulled up chairs to join our front yard think tank.

"It seems to me there are some good pharmaceuticals that can help quell this for you," said Dr. Dan, the trusty and recently retired psychiatrist. I talked to him about the medication I was taking—2020 was not a year to try to muscle through without help—and he approved.

"Maybe you can talk to your doctor about upping your dosage. See what that does. People really do find great relief."

"Also," Jean pointed out, "you aren't alone. You have the kids, and Charlotte can drive, right?"

"Totally," Martha responded.

"Maybe she can," I countered. "I have to think about it." The mother in me took over. Was it fair to ask this of her?

Charlotte is my sunshine kid who says yes to everything. If there is a task to do, she will jump in with both feet without looking. It has been my job, for the twenty-two years of her life, to slow her down, make her say what *she* wants and what *she* needs. On the flip side, Tobi, at twelve years old, has no problem saying what they need, with a clarity I sometimes envy. Tobi came out of the womb with an arched eyebrow and a constant need for alone time. I have a constant need to drag Tobi out of their room to watch *The Brady Bunch* and snuggle with me on the couch. I enjoy that Tobi takes work, it keeps me on my parenting toes. It also helps that Tobi is hilarious, calling themself "The Alpha of Comedy."

I roll my eyes, but Martha yells, "That's right! Tobi's the Alpha of Comedy!"

These kids are full of joy and full of laughs and wrestle like lion cubs despite their ten-year age gap. Taking them on this trip was, I believed, a once-in-a-lifetime experience.

Jean was right. Charlotte was the solution. I called her and explained about Martha leaving and that I was trying to decide if I should stay out in the RV. She listened and asked questions, mostly about the movie Martha was working on, which she thought sounded *SO COOL*. I had to come right out and ask her.

"Charlotte, do you have any interest in being my co-pilot, with the responsibility of driving the RV on large interstates for long periods of time? Think before you answer."

"Yes."

She hadn't thought about it at all.

"Charlotte, you didn't think about it at all."

"I know, but Mom. MOM. THIS IS THE TRIP OF A LIFETIME."

When Charlotte texts with me it is in all caps. *MOM. MOM. I AM PICKING UP MAKENNA AND WE ARE DRIVING TO THE BEACH AND I AM GOING TO BRING MY COLORING BOOKS AND PENCILS AND HAVE LUNCH FROM THE TACO PLACE AND IT WILL BE THE GREATEST DAY EVER.*

Even though we were talking on the phone, I knew her excitement for this trip was in all caps.

"Listen to me, child. This is not easy. You will have to train to drive the RV. You will have to learn how to dump the black and gray water. You will have to help me with the dogs and navigating and backing up and leveling and cooking and putting everything away. It's a lot. A LOT."

I added the sound of all caps so I was speaking her language.

"And you will seriously have to drive. I cannot do it alone. I think you can drive on highways, but it is not easy. It's heavy. You can only use the rear-view mirrors."

"YES."

"Charlotte."

"MOM."

"Wait. One question." She sounded serious. "Am I old enough to drive? I'm not even old enough to rent a car."

"Legally you can't rent a tiny Toyota Corolla until you're twenty-five, but at eighteen you can rent a thirty-foot RV and drive it anywhere in the continental United States."

"This is terrifying information."

"Agreed. Now. Can you please think about this for one more minute?"

There was a pause. A not quite long enough pause. I would call it perfunctory.

"I'm in. Let's do this! I have had FOMO over this trip all summer. I'm the only one who hasn't been in there." I detected a very slight whine. "Do we have to go straight back? Can we go somewhere cool?"

"We can go wherever we want. We just have to get back in time for Tobi to start school."

Now I was totally in over my head. Visions of me driving my

children straight over a cliff flashed momentarily. I pushed away fear and thought of the fun. This felt urgent. Important. I wanted to *be* the strong mom they both see when they look at me. I wanted Charlotte to have fun in the RV. I was desperate to prove to myself that I could do it, and even more to try to salvage some kind of fun for these two kids who were losing time in their precious youth to this stupid virus. Charlotte, without even knowing she was doing it, would help me through it.

I thought about all the places we could go. The safest route was to go the southern route through Texas. It avoided nearly all the mountain roads, which every other route home drove straight through because of the Rockies. We could manage the southern route.

I could manage it.

I could feel Charlotte's wheels turning.

And then:

"MOM. MOM. LET'S GO TO YELLOWSTONE."

Yellowstone. Where I'd white-knuckled in the passenger seat earlier in the summer while Martha drove on roads too narrow for a bike. Where there were grizzly bears and bison, and thermal burn pools of scientific awesomeness. Where every single landmark required a drive on a death-defying road. I knew I couldn't do it, but I wasn't going to tell her that. I gave her a solid and well-worn mother's answer.

"Maybe."

CHAPTER 14

THE ONLY WAY OUT
IS THROUGH

The RV trip was made slightly less daunting by the fact that I'd driven across the country several times before. My most recent cross-country trip was the last leg of a long journey, one that started in 1991 and ended in divorce. Some of that story is too delicate to tell, too maddening for the other people involved, and water under the bridge. The more fun part, anyway, is the trip.

In the school year wind-up of 2016, Charlotte graduated high school and Tobi finished second grade. Charlotte went to the definition of a groovy Southern California high school. She'd left her New York City public high school after her freshman year, when we moved to San Diego for a job opportunity. This move pulled Charlotte out of New York just as Charlotte had found a boyfriend and a solid group of friends called "The Blob." They hung out in Union Square and frequented the Strand bookstore, where they would flirt and laugh and run around in the miles of books, and then they'd eat pizza and take the subway home. I watched in awe, feeling so square with my Cincinnati upbringing. Hers was like a John Hughes film.

In New York City Charlotte enjoyed a freedom I knew would be hard to maintain in California (at least until she could drive), so I searched high and low for the *perfect* school (no pressure). The public school options were not a good fit for her, all of them just so gigantic. I found Charlotte a little private school near the beach. They were excited to have her, and I knew Charlotte would be taken with the modern Southern California campus which sprawled over the hills of the hippy (but uber-expensive) beach town of Encinitas. Surfing was a Phys Ed option, which was hilarious to us, such a far cry from the Phys Ed she was used to in New York City, which mainly involved variations of running around orange cones in a fenced paved lot. In every way it was a massive departure from the dilapidated building that housed her competitive New York school, but the kids looked interesting and similar to her tribe of New York buddies.

Once in San Diego she initially struggled to find her footing, but then fell headfirst into the drama department, met her people, and never looked back. The one exception was her New York City boyfriend, Rhys, a great kid with willing parents, who traveled back and forth for visits and kept the romance alive for another several years. Going back to New York City meant a reunion, and then an internship at a farm upstate where she and Rhys would finally have time together, pulling carrots.

Tobi was finishing up second grade and had little memory of New York City. I was excited to get them back there and teach them the finer points of playground hopping in Central Park, something akin to a pub crawl, but instead of drinking think popsicles and swing sets.

I packed between school drop-off and pick-up, in various-sized boxes from Home Depot. Twenty-four years of things bought together were raggedly divided. For my part, I left the Southern California ranch that I'd painted and decorated, the pool I'd insisted on as a nod to my dad, the bikes and ski boots, the books and linens.

I left a large part of my heart. I left memories: the good, and then the very bad.

Many friends came and helped. They kept me going. They moved me faster as the deadline approached and my sorrow and anxiety grew, side by side, paired with excitement and hope. *Come From Away* had been a solid hit everywhere it went, but New York City critics are tough. Our sweet musical about the kindness of community could easily get dumped on, especially in a crowded field of top-notch shows coming to Broadway. If it hit, I was golden. At least for a while. If it closed, I was back to the same reason I'd left New York in the first place—the relentless rejection of showbiz. And now I had two kids counting on my paycheck, a new kind of pressure for me.

Martha was my oasis. Her tiny L-shaped apartment in Midtown already felt like home, and when I visited, we rarely left each other's side, making the four hundred square feet feel easily manageable. Now I was arriving with two kids and a cat, making the occupancy grand total three cats and four humans. As a stage manager, Martha is used to organizing small spaces, but even this proved daunting. I sent her updates and questions as I packed.

French press. Bring with me or Goodwill? She'd ask 50 questions about it. Color, size, how often I used it. She'd compare it with what she had and then respond:

I think we're good with my one-cupper.

But Martha loves a garage sale, and my divorce division of goods was like a garage sale on steroids, with the perfect price point of free. Nearly every time I'd offer something up I'd get a breezy text back: *Sure, why not? Bring it!* I wondered if she had secret storage in her apartment to hold all this stuff, but I pushed it aside. We'd figure it out.

I wrapped up vases that were wedding presents, rummaged through the kitchen to take only my favorite or most nostalgic things. I would pack six boxes in an hour and then sit and look at old pictures for a half a day, weary and sad, getting little done. My mother had just died, and she seemed to be with me as I packed every box. Not having my parents to lean on was brand-new. My father was now rudderless without my mom, lost in a memory care home, sad and mad, and too far gone to be there for me. In a different life, I would have called my parents every hour on the hour to report on the latest. My mother would have flown to San Diego to help me pack.

I allowed myself to feel relieved they did not know all of this was happening. My mom died proud of me, but she was a Catholic and a conservative, leaving me with no belief that—as much as she loved me—she could have ever accepted my new life. By that I mean both the divorce and Martha. A double whammy. *Yes*, I thought to myself. *It's a blessing she's not here.* Martha, dynamic and full bodied in presence and personality, managed to single-handedly fill much of the void. In some deeper place, beyond the fear, I knew my parents would be happy I had her.

As I packed, I bombarded Martha with pictures; of the kids as babies, of my parents, of old headshots of mine. A time capsule viewing of the life that was headed her way.

By the end, I had a small but full storage unit in a baking-hot desert complex on the aptly named Leaping Lizards Road. I hired some guys from the Home Depot parking lot to help me load and unload the U-Haul I'd rented, and as I watched as the door rolled down on the boxes of Playbills and kids' toys and dishware that I could not bear to part with, but I could not fit in the car, I wondered what would happen to it. To me. Would I stay with Martha? Would I stay in New York City if Martha and I broke up? What would I do if *Come From Away* closed?

Where would the contents of my storage unit land? I shut the door and moved on.

Martha was the lone buoy bobbing in distant New York City. Ready or not, here we come.

◆ ◆ ◆

I planned the trip along the fastest route; the second most southern route through Arizona, and on up through Oklahoma and on to Ohio and finally to New York and Martha.

I mapped it out with a precision previously unknown to me. This was it. My very first venture out into the world as a mom on my own. I had six days of solo parenting. If there was a screwup, it was mine to handle. I told myself this was precious time with my kids, and we needed it after a year of such sadness and hurt. I was desperate to not only successfully drive there, but to make it epic.

I was also broke. I had taken a loan from work to be paid back once I was making a substantial paycheck, which was still many months away. *Come From Away* had an extended out-of-town trial period prior to Broadway, first in Seattle and San Diego and then later in Washington, DC, Newfoundland, Toronto, and then (finally) Broadway. The constant worries plagued me: *What if the show flops? How will I pay that money back?*

For now, at least, I was okay, I just needed to be as frugal as possible. This was the first time since college I'd been responsible for my own finances, and it was frightening. I left college thousands of dollars in debt, and it took me years and management by others to get out of it. I'd never trusted myself to manage money, and frankly, I feared it. Fortunately, I had one big ace up my sleeve; when *Come From Away* played Seattle, we were housed in a Hilton for about seven weeks. The producers paid for it, but we were allowed to collect the travel points. I had enough points to stay in Hiltons free of charge for the entire trip, including one big splurge on the night of the Tony Awards, where the kids and I could stay in a resort-type property in Sedona, Arizona. Super-fancy.

I had the nights booked, the car packed, the GPS programmed, and two excited kids. We left early on the morning of June 12th. I took a picture for Martha just before we left the driveway, and my breezy smile and sunglasses did not reflect my fear. If the picture could talk it would have said, *Oh God, please don't dump me. I'm coming with my kids. Please don't dump me.*

Martha's text response was swift and sure.

"You cuties! Get over here!"

Followed immediately by another text.

"Wow. That car looks full."

She was right. We were packed to the gills.

Martha lived in an L-shaped studio in the middle of Manhattan, and shared the space with her long-time cat roommate, Dot. Martha is almost intimidatingly good at taking care of animals, a real pet whisperer, but she hadn't spent a lot of time around kids. She's cautious around anyone younger than the production assistants on her show, unlike me, who just moves in and starts firing questions and using my hand as a puppet to make them laugh. I always have gum in my purse and usually a toy. I can paint a kid's face to look like a cat with any makeup on hand. Kids are easy for me. For Martha it was much scarier and slower. A sample of Martha's opinion: "I would never want kids. Never. Ever. And I would never be with a person who had kids."

Others might be nervous. I thought it was cute. Mostly because I didn't believe her one iota.

I explained, "Martha. The kids are like Dot. You feed them, you play with them, they sleep. You've got this."

She sent a lot of funny videos of hamsters eating celery. My kids loved her immediately.

Martha's main priority was dividing her studio apartment with floor-to-ceiling curtains that could also slide in for privacy. She enlisted her best buddy Joey to help, and they made a complicated rigging system that divided the apartment into sections. Martha was working twelve to fourteen hours a day at this point on a Broadway revival of *The Crucible* and time was not on her side. As the trip progressed and our arrival was imminent, I got the impression that Martha was not really ready for us. And I wondered about the attention to curtains vs. emptying a drawer or two.

"Mar, not for nothing, but we are getting close. I know you are busy, but you'd better hop to it, Sis."

I was a little disappointed by her procrastination. I'd done nothing but work. This trip was the end of months of brutal transition of divorce and the pain of losing my mother. I'd spent the better part of the year delivering variations of shocking news: "My mom died. My dad is now in a home. We are selling my parents' house. I'm getting divorced. I'm dating a woman."

I'm a strong person, but my year of 2015-2016 would rattle even the strongest. I was, by this point, almost a shell of myself. Beaten down and sad, needing something to anchor me. I'd put all my faith in Martha and me being together and *Come From Away* being a hit.

I'd pushed all my chips in. New York, Martha, and *Come From Away* were my payout. As she hung curtains, we barreled on, my foot on the gas pedal.

◆ ◆ ◆

Day one of the drive was critical. This would set the tone for the rest of the trip, and I wanted something fabulous. I wanted memories for a lifetime. I wanted the kids to see how very capable I was without any help. Mommy is okay, I reminded myself again and again. Mommy is okay.

The shwanky resort in Sedona, Arizona, was to serve two goals.

Watch the Tony Awards.

Hike to a Sedona vortex.

After a beautiful and uneventful drive, we checked in to our lush one-bedroom suite, put on bathing suits, and headed to the multi-level resort pool. I love a resort pool. What could be better? Waterfalls and swim-up grottos? Check, check, check. Fun for all, a slam dunk.

Tobi and I swam under a cool waterfall that had a ledge to sit on. We enjoyed the velocity of the water and the freedom of the moment for a moment, peacefully sitting under there, talking and enjoying the echo of our voices. Then Tobi suddenly stood up and smashed their head into the ceiling, not blacking out but hurting themself enough that a medic was called, and I worried for the rest of the night that they had a concussion.

They were more traumatized than hurt, but considering it was our first night and supposed to be the *perfect night*, it was wildly upsetting. I did not let on to the kids. I soothed Tobi and held an ice pack in place. But I was mad at myself and panicked. My deepest fears took over. *Turn around. You can't do this. Day one and Tobi almost had to go to the hospital. Way to go, you frigging incompetent idiot. This is karma for ruining your children's lives.*

I ordered room service for the Tony Awards, which seemed like a win until I saw that the bill topped $90 and, again, my inner voice screamed. *Too expensive! You have no job! You cannot budget! You will end up homeless.* The homeless fear was a real one. I'd passed a mother on a local road in San Diego with a cardboard sign that said *Need food for kids. Many thanks. Trying to be a good mom.*

It haunted me. I could imagine writing that sign. If I ever aired these fears, I knew people would talk about "potential" and how I always "land on my feet." No one was worrying about me, which meant *no one was worrying about me.* I worried enough for everyone. I could imagine begging for food. I could feel it nipping at my toes. It never felt that far away. Even though I'd had a life of privilege, I had no savings to fall back on, and no parents to bail me out. I had one thing, the car, and I often checked the Kelly Blue Book value of it, just to see how much I could get in an absolute emergency. Not much, I'd concluded. I'd applied to be an Uber driver in San Diego a few months back and was turned down because my car wasn't in good enough shape.

The kids and I watched the Tony Awards, and it started out fun but rapidly became the most boring Tony Awards ever presented as Hamilton won award after award. I watched and wondered if there was any chance that I could possibly be on the Tony Awards show with *Come From Away* the following year. Charlotte looked over and gave me a wink. "That'll be you next year, Mama!"

I sat and held an ice pack on Tobi's head, looking at sweet Charlotte, who was always just so willing and positive. From my current vantage point, a future where I appeared on the Tony Awards seemed like a pipe dream. I worried all that was ahead of us was disappointment, but I nodded weakly and smiled. "I hope so, kid. I hope so."

We slept well and Tobi woke up feeling much better. We had a long drive ahead of us, to Amarillo, Texas. But before that I had one last stop in Sedona. I wanted to take the kids to a vortex.

Sedona vortexes are famous energy fields of healing. The entire area is thought to be highly spiritual, but there are four distinct areas where the energy is thought to be the strongest. I knew we had a long drive, eleven hours in the car that day at least, but I felt it was essential we give the energy vortex a go. If any mom and two kids needed an energy renewal, it was us. I picked the easiest and closest one and ignored the voice in my head *This is bullshit and not real. Get on the road. You are so stupid. You have a long drive ahead of you. You know better.*

On top of that, Tobi didn't want to go. They were deeply into a video game and cozy in the backseat, adding to my guilt in upending their life. I was repeatedly asking them to do things they didn't want to do. They met my eye in the rear-view mirror.

"Can I stay in the car?"

"No."

It was already about 102 degrees in the early morning heat. "It's too hot to stay in the car. Besides, it's a short walk up a hill. No big deal."

Tobi was silent. Mad.

"Please," I said. "Do it for me."

That didn't appeal to them either, but eventually they were convinced. Charlotte, who is long-legged and had a season of volleyball muscles to propel her, bounded up and tried to engage Tobi to join. We got to the top. It wasn't pretty, but we got there.

There were a couple of other groups taking in the view and the vibe, and Charlotte took off with her camera. I sat on the rock, tried to calm my mind, and waited for something to happen. Nothing good came. My mind raced with worry that we were running late, that I would be destitute, that Martha would leave me, that I'd ruined everyone's lives, the usual.

I laid down on the rock and felt the warmth through my back but opened my eyes when I felt a shade and a presence. Tobi was above me, standing over me, furious. They were so mad, and looked so unlike themself, I took a picture.

And then Tobi started yelling at me.

"I do not want to be here. I TOLD you. Everyone makes me do things I DO NOT WANT TO DO."

It went on from there. Tobi became hysterical. They ran from me. I caught up with them and had no other choice but to hold them down. I held them down on that red rock and told them to scream and cry. There was so much to release. Their parents were getting divorced, their grandmother had died, they were stuck in a car heading to their mom's new girlfriend's tiny apartment in a city they didn't remember. It was hot. Charlotte looked on, wide-eyed. Wanting to do something, but not wanting to get involved.

I continued coaching Tobi. "Do it. Cry it out. You're right. This all sucks and I'm sorry. Look at me. I am so, so, so sorry."

Tobi cried and cried. I wrapped my arms around them, and within moments Charlotte joined our circle and I apologized to her, too.

I reminded them, again, that this was not their fault. This was me, and my life, and choices I was making for my own happiness that would make us all unhappy for a while. I explained that I believed we'd all been unhappy for a long time.

"I haven't," Tobi said.

"I have," Charlotte said quietly. And then she cried, too. I looked at my beautiful kids, both with watery eyes and open hearts.

"I'm sorry. This is all my fault. It's not yours, and there is no way to fix it. The only way out is through. We must keep moving ahead."

Charlotte repeated me. "The only way out is through."

"Yes." I looked at Tobi. "Can you do it?" Tobi didn't say anything, and instead hugged me, which said enough.

We sat like that for a long time, breathing and looking at the landscape.

I made my kids a vow.

"I can't promise you this will be perfect. I can't. I don't have a crystal ball. But I promise you to try as hard as I can. I promise to work hard. I promise to tell you the truth. I promise to take care of you no matter what. I'm scared, but I'm hopeful. Can you be hopeful with me?"

We agreed to be hopeful. Then we laughed about the stupid vortexes and how we would never do it again because they were so stupid and didn't work.

"A waste of time. We felt nothing," Charlotte said as we hiked down. And then we piled back into the car and drove to Amarillo, Texas. Tobi sang "I love you" to me to a made-up tune for most of Arizona, continuing it well into Texas. Charlotte sang, "You're Driving Me Crazy" to Tobi for nearly the same amount of time. We were in good shape. Better and better, state by state.

Meanwhile, in New York City, Martha was still mid-curtain. "I'm hemming them!" When I asked *how* she was hemming them she said, "With black duct tape."

She always chose function over beauty.

A few hours later there was a text.

"Dude. The bed's here. It's about a million pieces. I don't think I can do this."

Martha had ordered a bunk bed for the kids. It was white and she'd purchased pink sheets with flowers on them as guided by Tobi, prompting Martha to say, "This is the girliest thing that's ever been in this apartment. Besides you, of course, my darling."

Quick aside: Look at your nails.

According to Martha, if you look at your nails with your hand flat and palm facing the ground, you are girlie. If you look at your nails by facing your palm up and curling your nails towards you, you are butch. You can imagine how Martha and I fare in this test.

Martha put away the duct tape, pulled out her power tools, called Joey back over, and they built the bed. My kids thought all of this was hilarious and checked via FaceTime through most of Texas. Martha enjoys being a showman and narrating her life, so it worked perfectly. I just kept driving, delighted to hear my kids laughing. I knew she was freaking out and not ready for us, but they didn't.

◆ ◆ ◆

When we arrived in Amarillo and finally pulled up to the hotel, it was around midnight. The hotel, called the Home 2 Suites, was alone in a vast parking lot and appeared to be still under construction, with protective plastic still covering the sliding doors to the lobby. We got out and the kids charged in, sick of the car. They were delighted by the bright colors, the weird plastic couches. They pored over the locked refrigerators full of small cartons of milk to go with the boxes of crappy cereal for the free breakfast.

"There is a make-your-own-waffle station!" Charlotte announced. They high-fived.

When we opened the door to the long hotel room, we discovered curtains. Tons of curtains, all set up to divide the room into sections. We immediately shot videos of the kids sliding the curtains all over the room to divide it up.

"Just like your apartment, Martha!!!"

Tobi pulled out all of the Littlest Pet Shop pets from their bag, pulled a curtain shut, and started to play. Charlotte draped herself on the couch, pulled the curtain shut, and called Rhys to tell him about the *coolest hotel ever*.

"It's a motel!" I clarified. The Sedona resort had cost me over half my coveted points, and here we were in the cheapest hotel, sorry, *motel* of the trip and the kids were begging me to stay longer. The waffles the next morning were a highlight of the trip, but nothing beat the sliding curtains.

We had other events, like a massive thunderstorm that coincided with the very first time Charlotte took the wheel. After days and days of driving, I was tired, and she'd been begging to drive. She was a fairly new driver, but I'd relented. It was flat and Illinois. We were on a highway. What could happen? A torrential downpour and nearly no visibility happened.

I talked her through it, slowly, carefully, not allowing her to see my concern, and we pulled off at the first exit as the semi-trucks repeatedly drenched the car. We went into a gas station to get a drink and wait out the storm, and within moments the gas station lost power. Someone played the weather report to follow a nearby tornado. In a room full of anxious adults, Tobi found a book, sat down on the floor, and read, not anxious at all. When it was safe, I'd tell them, and until then they'd read a book, trusting me to keep them safe. I started to trust me, too.

By the time we arrived in New York City, the excitement was real for all of us. Charlotte turned on Frank Sinatra's version of "New York, New York."

Except for Martha. She was building that bed right up until the last minute, even while we were in the Lincoln Tunnel, and kept joking, "You can slow down a little if you want . . . ." She was still working long days and exhausted. I felt bad but it was also a little mixed with *uh hey, you really need to be ready because I've got my whole life in this car, and these kids can't think you don't want them here.*

Martha's apartment building had a parking garage underneath and when we arrived I sent a text, a little joke from *Come From Away.* "Safe and sound on the ground in . . . .your garage. Come down and get us!!"

She came through the door in full Martha fashion, bellowing, "Hello! Hello! You made it!" and kissing me more than we probably should in front of the kids, but they just laughed. She looked us all over, paying special attention to the "Grab it" toy Tobi had picked up from the Cracker Barrel gift shop. "That will work very well for your mother. You know she's short. She can't reach things." The kids loved when Martha called me short. That led to an impromptu challenge from Charlotte that she was taller than Martha, with Tobi squealing, "She is! Charlotte's taller!"

Meanwhile I was slowly unpacking the car and organizing. Martha turned around and saw the growing pile of goods and seemed shocked. I noticed the small, gray granny cart she'd brought down to help move things up. It would fit maybe two gallons of milk, max. We looked at each other and she said, "This is all going up into my apartment?"

I wasn't even a quarter of the way unloading the car. I stood my ground. "Yes, Martha. You know, I actually moved out. Like . . . out. Like . . . we're moving in."

"Right, of course! No problem. I see that now."

She crossed her arms and thought. I had no idea what she was going to say. I was immediately flooded with guilt and worry, my brain spinning like a top. *What was I thinking? This is too much. This isn't what she wanted. It's over. The kids. Oh my God. Homeless. I'll rent an apartment. I'll never qualify, I have no job right now. I'll find a Home 2 Motel. The kids love that. We'll live there forever—*

She interrupted my brain hurricane with a simple statement.

"We'll need to make several trips to get all this upstairs." She looked at the kids and started directing them.

"Charlotte, you grab the paintings, Tobi, you grab the pillows. Here we go."

The kids grabbed things and stepped in line.

"Isn't Dot going to be surprised to see all of this?" She laughed. We followed her in.

CHAPTER 15

MA

Let me be real for a minute. It super sucked that Martha had to leave to film *Diana*, and I made her feel as horrid as I could about it by constantly listing all the ways her leaving made my life harder.

"Oh *great*," I'd say. "Now the propane is out. Another thing I don't know how to do."

Or: "Now there is a HURRICANE coming. Awesome. Perfect timing." Martha, meanwhile, was already swamped with emails and loads of work stuff by the time we drove into San Diego, where she was set to fly out two days later. I made ambitious to-do lists for her ("PLEASE CLEAN OUT THE GARAGE/BASEMENT OF ALL YOUR STUFF SO I DO NOT HAVE TO DO THAT, TOO") and she did lots of laundry to get away from me. Martha's other response to my anxiety was to train Young Jedi Charlotte within an inch of her life on her role in the RV. Martha regularly hired production assistants and interns who were Charlotte's age, and Charlotte is often an intern, so it was a successful match-up from the get-go. They did driving lessons around the La Jolla Playhouse parking lot, then in wider circles around San Diego, and finally out onto the highway before Martha enthusiastically deemed her "trained."

I was still nervous. But I knew Martha did not give false praise even when a person might really want that from her, so if she said Charlotte was ready, she was ready.

"Oh, I never got around to teaching her to dump the tanks. But you can do it." She laughed as I grimaced. "Just because you don't *want* to do it doesn't mean you can't do it."

"We'll see about that," I replied. I knew I was being a brat. She did another load of laundry and left me on the couch, moody, watching *Handmaid's Tale* on my phone. Some sound advice: if you are looking to cheer up, do *not* watch *Handmaid's Tale*.

One bright spot: Martha decided to take Ethel back to New York with her, reasoning it was better for an elderly kitty to have one plane ride rather than another two weeks in the RV, and I agreed, totally. When I asked what we'd do about Ethel when she went into quarantine with the cast and crew for the movie, Martha cheerily explained that she'd take Ethel with her.

"She'll be good company!"

On Martha's last night we drove down to La Jolla Shores, a beautiful beach where Martha and I had many memories, and we took a walk along the water. I cried a lot and apologized a lot and Martha understood. After six months of being by each other's side for every moment of every day, we would be separated for seven weeks, marking the longest span of time we'd ever spent apart. I was sad for her to leave. She was sad to leave the RV. Everything was a little less fun and a lot quieter with Martha gone. Sparky and I moped on the couch for a day, and then set off to the grocery store to stock up for the kids.

◆ ◆ ◆

MY KIDS. I WAS GOING TO GET MY KIDS!

If this were an iPhone, I'd do that thing where you can send the message with fireworks, kapow kapow! They piled in the RV with youth and gusto and laughter, easing my mind and making all my decisions feel like I was doing things EXACTLY RIGHT. I could even feel my mother, who I'd imagined would be against this idea, give me a high five and tell me I'd made the right choice. Kapow! Kapow!

As Martha landed in New York we hit the road. As it would happen, we were driving straight through the hottest part of the United States in the hottest time of the year, driving across the desert southwest from San Diego to Las Vegas. I'd heard the tires can blow in extreme heat, so we opted to drive at night, pulling onto the Las Vegas Strip somewhere around 1:00 a.m. I wasn't tired, I wasn't scared, I was simply happy to have the chirping of my two kids as they commented on everything. We'd lived in Las Vegas for a year when Charlotte was eight, while I did *Avenue Q* at the Wynn Casino, and Charlotte pointed out everything she could remember as we drove.

"Ma, why do I remember that?" she asked as we pulled up to the Bellagio.

"You had a school field trip there to look at the artwork."

"At a casino?"

"Vegas is weird."

We sat in front of the Bellagio, rolled down the windows, and watched the famous water fountain show right there from the RV as it performed for us, an audience of three. Then we pulled into Sam's KOA and Casino, parked and leveled, Tobi walked the dogs, and I taught Charlotte how to dump the tanks. All-around badassery.

I really wanted to drive through Utah and Colorado to see Zion, Bryce, Moab, Arches, and Rocky National Park. There was an entire route Martha and I'd skipped when we'd turned around in Montana. I had it mapped out, campsites booked, the whole nine yards, and then I-70 was totally shut down due to a massive fire that basically eliminated any chance that we could go that way. And along the southern route there was a hurricane headed for Texas.

I channeled my inner GPS and we rerouted, adding about a thousand miles onto the trip, and we headed where Charlotte wanted to go, back to Yellowstone, my third time in a month. We did fun camp-y things on the way there, like biking in Zion on the valley floor at night because it was too hot to do it during the day. Then Charlotte drove us into Idaho, and we camped on a creek and started a s'mores-making competition that lasted every night for the rest of the trip.

You've heard about Yellowstone already, so let me leave you with these three additional specifics.

1. I drove that park like a boss and it's not easy. Part of what makes it not easy is the proclivity for wildlife to bound out onto the middle of the road with no notice. Martha and I had learned this the hard way one night when we were driving back from the Lamar Valley, about a ninety-minute drive in the pitch black, and we rounded the corner at about fifty miles an hour to find a bison standing in the middle of the road. Another night it was a pronghorn, which we narrowly missed. When I was there with the kids, I was driving to our campsite and passing the river. Next thing I knew, a wolf with a large fish in his mouth ran out of the river and crossed our path as it bounded for the woods. People watch for wolves with all kinds of sophisticated equipment in Yellowstone (it's a good story, how they reintroduced the wolves) and I almost had one as a grill ornament. I braked so hard half of the kitchen flew into the dinette, and then the kids and I sat there, stunned, making sure we'd really seen what we'd thought we'd seen. It was incredible.

2. All Tobi wanted was snow. It was the end of August and in the world of Yellowstone, snow was possible and even predicted during the two nights we camped there, with the temperatures going down into the 30s, which, we all agreed, was bananas considering that we'd just spent a night in Zion where it had hit 116 a few days before. We never did wake up to snow, but I am happy to report that Tobi got some flurries later in the day as we drove out the steep and winding eastern entrance into Cody, Wyoming. Because what makes a steep and winding drive more fun in an RV? Snow! Woot woot! Charlotte turned on Aretha Franklin's greatest hits and she sang us up and down those mountains with "R-E-S-P-E-C-T."

3. Charlotte decided she wanted to try her butch muscles by chopping wood with a small hatchet Martha'd left behind. I was thrilled because we were out of smaller pieces of wood. When I looked over Charlotte was in a flannel shirt and Birkenstocks, taking a picture of herself swinging the hatchet. She split one piece of wood, and then she split.

As in: never swung that hatchet again. Not exactly Paul Bunyan, my elder child, but she looked cute on social media.

◆ ◆ ◆

We powered through Wyoming and headed into South Dakota for the one other thing Tobi wanted to see: Mount Rushmore. It was right around this time that I got a phone call from Martha, who had completed her two-week quarantine in our apartment and had just arrived to check in to the hotel where the entire *Diana* cast was quarantining while they recorded the cast album.

"Am I on speaker phone?" It was a fair question. If Martha called, the kids wanted to yell all of the things we'd seen and done that day.

"You are."

"HI MARTHA," Charlotte yelled. "CRAZY HORSE IS CRAZY HUGE."

"MARTHA," Tobi yelled. "CHARLOTTE TORE HER PINKIE TOE OPEN AND RUINED HER BIRKENSTOCKS WITH BLOOD."

"Do you want me to take you off?" I asked.

"I do," she said, and I did.

"Sorry, honey. What can I say? They love you. Did I tell you we slept in Deadwood last night?" I started to yammer on with all the things that felt urgent to say.

"Hey. Listen to me." Her voice was serious. "I tested positive for Covid."

I felt like I was falling. Like I'd been sucked into a vortex. After all this time, after all these precautions. How? I stayed outwardly calm and breezy. Charlotte was sitting right next to me, and Tobi always seemed deep into their video game but heard everything from any vantage point.

"Okay. Tell me more. Are you alright?"

"Yes. I was negative yesterday, but when I woke up this morning, I had a sore throat. Scratchy. I mentioned it to the nurses when I went down for my second round of testing and they had me drink orange juice, which is adorable. Then they just came up and told me. The test was positive."

"What happens now?"

"I was supposed to be released this afternoon so I can set everything up in the rehearsal room. Now I can't be released until they run another test to see if this test is still positive—or wait—maybe they run this one again—I can't remember. Basically, Ethel and I are locked in our room. It's a disaster."

"But maybe it will come back with a different result?" I was trying to speak in code, but Charlotte was already tuned in, mouthing, *Is she ok?* I nodded an adamant *yes*.

"I don't know. I just don't. I am totally freaked out. They want me to go home, which I think is a terrible idea." She was crying. "I said I wouldn't go home. I cried on the phone with my boss. I'm *fine*. I had a little sore throat. It's nothing. I really don't think I have Covid."

"Oh honey." I talked to her more openly, knowing Charlotte knew what I was saying, and soon I had Tobi's little face up there, too, both of them intensely listening to me as I tried to talk in code. It's hard to keep a secret in an RV.

Martha started to get a series of emails and ended the call with an abrupt "Honey, I've got to go. I'll call you back."

I looked over at my worried kids.

"She's okay."

Tobi demands facts. "Tell me everything."

"I am only a little bit worried. She is in very good care with a top-notch medical team. She is in quarantine in a comfy hotel room."

"And what else?" Tobi demanded. "What do they do next?"

"Well, they rerun the test and keep testing her, and I assume at some point she'll be let out of her room." I left out a lot, but I gave them enough information that they felt part of it.

But I was worried. There wasn't a single other thing I could do for Martha. She'd willingly taken an airplane and put herself at risk, so my kids didn't have to. I figured, at this point, the best thing I could do would be to have fun with the kids and get them home safely.

We kept going.

Every day was a series of new decisions. What's the best route? Where should we sleep? Are we cooking over a fire? Are we grabbing takeout and eating in a parking lot? Is there enough water in the tank for a shower? Do we slow down and see more, or do we barrel on as fast as we can so we can be closer to Martha? Could I do anything for her? I was winging it.

I really wanted to detour to De Smet, South Dakota, to see the Ingalls homestead, but it felt irresponsible—it was one hundred miles north, completely rerouting us. The kids did not want to go, wanting to get to Cincinnati faster to reunite with our Cincinnati family. But when in the hell would I ever get this close to De Smet again? I'd already sacrificed a detour back in Missouri where I'd floated the idea of seeing another Laura Ingalls Wilder home on Rocky Ridge Farm, where she and her daughter Rose had written the series. I'd been sad to miss it, but it wasn't like the books were set there, just written there. But here in South Dakota? This was it. The real-life setting for bonnets and braids and horses and Half-pint—all of it. *The Little House on the Prairie* series was deep in my DNA. Much to my chagrin, neither of my kids had caught the bug, instead choosing Harry Potter as their go-to childhood hero. I get it. He's cool. But the Ingalls were *real*, and their homestead was up the road a piece and I wanted to drag them kicking and screaming, to do something I wanted to do. They should respect me! Little pitchers have big ears! Children should be seen and not heard! All this excellent parenting advice—and more!—can be found in the pages of Laura Ingalls Wilder's books. Surely, *surely* I could force them to like it.

I reminded myself that it was okay for kids to try things their parents liked, even when it was weird. I remember my mom loved this old-fashioned gum, Choward's Violet, and any time we saw it in a store, which was usually on vacation to someplace like Pigeon Forge, Tennessee, in a store that also sold tiny cokes in bottles and moccasins, she'd buy it and give me a stick. To her it tasted like happy days of childhood. To me it tasted like chewing on a lavender candle. I chewed it for her, to make the moment happy. I said I loved it for her, I would even happily chew it now just as a reminder of her. But in reality I couldn't wait to rip the wrapper off my Watermelon Hubba Bubba and wash away all the waxy lavender flavor. "The whole car stinks like fake watermelon!" my mother would complain. *Exactly*, I would think.

I knew the Ingalls homestead was my Choward's Violet and my kids wanted Hubba Bubba. But we were going anyway.

We started the day in Mitchell, South Dakota, where we impulsively followed a sign that said *The World's Largest Corn Palace!*

Largest? Were there others?

Palace? Really? That's a big statement.

We had to go see.

Charlotte was "TOTALLY INTO IT."

Tobi asked if they could stay in the RV, which was usually as close to a yes as I was going to get. I hoped the Corn Palace was possibly groovy enough to warrant an RV exit.

We'd spent the night in a KOA in Mitchell, just a few miles from this famous palace, after a long, flat, cornfield-filled drive from Deadwood, South Dakota. The day had been action-packed, driving through Deadwood and all its history, a quick visit to Mt. Rushmore, and then swinging by the shockingly gigantic work-in-progress Wild Horse Monument. There was a fear of South Dakota in mid-August of 2020 because a bunch of bikers had gathered, maskless and proud, in Sturgess, SD, and made it a super-spreader event. We drove through Sturgess and saw too many American flags to count. We finally arrived in Mitchell quite late, after 11:00 p.m., which is super rude in KOA etiquette, as we were told by the host who came out to reprimand us as we circled the lot looking for the spot I'd reserved. To be fair, it was pitch black and surrounded by corn. A corn maze for RVs.

We were trying to make it all the way to my friend Linda's driveway in Wisconsin on the day of the Corn Palace, and I'd lightly mentioned the possibility of the Ingalls homestead but had not committed. It was about two hours out of the way, which I would do if it was a place the kids wanted to see, but to ask them to do it for me felt like too much.

So, I'd started the day with donuts and a corn palace. Everybody loves a donut and a corn palace. And I am not above a bribe.

Turns out, the corn palace was basically a multipurpose building in the middle of a tiny town that was covered with specially grown corn and local grasses. And unavailable due to Covid-19 restrictions. Tobi got out and took long looks at the amazing murals outside. It also housed my favorite gift shop of the entire trip, and we bought it out. Charlotte enjoyed acting as a reporter for her Instagram page by hosting an interview (with herself) using the corncob beer bottle opener magnet as a microphone. I enjoyed that even the souvenirs in the gift shop, much like the palace itself, had multiple uses. And just yesterday Martha had been telling me how much her podiatrist enjoyed her corn socks, picked out for her by Tobi.

Once we'd stocked up on all things corn, we hopped back into the RV and decided to drive to the Ingalls' place. The kids had both read enough of the Little House books to know where we were going, but as we approached, it became clear that the real excitement was for me.

"MOM," Charlotte explained. "YOU HAVE LOVED THIS YOUR WHOLE LIFE. WE HAVE TO GO." Still, I was hesitant.

"Tobs? What say you?"

Tobi didn't look up from playing Animal Crossing but asked if there would be Wi-Fi.

"I need to sell my peaches to buy a fishing pole." With that, I got a text from Martha. Tobi read it out loud. "Feeling fine. Rehearsal starts today. Running it on Zoom from my hotel room."

Charlotte laughed. "Martha is my spirit animal." We all felt better. I looked at the kids. "OK. Let's do this."

I set a time limit of forty-five minutes, tops, at the Ingalls place, and pointed our wagon north.

As I drove the RV through the beautiful waving prairies of South Dakota, I thought about my parents, aching for them. My life before the pandemic had been so busy, I'd barely had time to mourn them. During the pandemic I'd returned to my hometown, always aware that I was finally home for a long period of time, but now my parents were gone. I'd driven Martha and the kids past the house I grew up in, to the mausoleum where my parents' ashes were enclosed, telling them I'd put in a lipstick I wore in *Come From Away* with my mother, because she loved to take my lipsticks. Every day we threw the ball for Sparky on the giant lawn of the Hyde Park Observatory, where we'd held my dad's memorial in 2017. He hadn't lasted long without my mother. We spent long days and nights with my brother and his family and visited my sister and her husband Tony on their porch. Our Airbnb had been across the street from Zips, a cozy bar where my parents went for hamburgers every Friday night with their best friends, and those same best friends came for a porch visit, telling Martha all about my mom and dad. Martha never knew them, and Tobi was young when they died, so only Charlotte and I had memories of them. To make up for it, I immersed us in their world.

On the RV trip, I thought of them often, but now that Martha was working and it was just me and the kids, it felt like my parents were so close to me that I could reach out and touch them. I wanted to call them and regale them with stories of our day. I wanted to describe the corn palace and get bored as my dad would go on and on about how they built it. I wanted to describe the gift shop to my mom and not tell her I'd bought her an ornament, as I did in every gift shop, but she would know me well enough to know it was coming.

Only my mom and dad could truly understand the meaning of seeing Laura Ingalls Wilder's homestead. I'd reread the books so many times they had fallen apart at the seams. I finally had to toss them in the garbage and ask for a new box set for Christmas. My parents would find me up a tree in a bonnet, reading. I thought of Half-pint and Caroline and Charles, who lived near each other for most of Laura's life. Even as an adult she followed her Pa to Florida on a money-making scheme that fell through.

I had moved away from my parents. I had my own dreams. I had my own kids.

I had a wagon that I'd driven around the country, we'd seen wildlife up close, and we'd cooked over a fire. I was Ma and Pa and Laura all wrapped up in one.

As I lumbered north in our thirty-foot wagon on wheels, the kids stayed close to me. Charlotte brought me coffee and Tobi sat in the middle, between us. The kids had a loud *Hamilton* sing-along, which I'd interrupt to point out hawks floating through the cloudless sky. None of us could get over the wind gusts that blew our little home back and forth, the grasses waving in unison with us.

The kids loved the Ingalls homestead from the moment we drove in, the dirt road deeply pocketed with rain-filled ponds, causing the RV to rock back and forth in a thrilling and terrifying way. Tobi tossed their video game and phone aside, and quickly became adamant that we weren't *ever* leaving.

"Why didn't you tell me this place was *so awesome?*" I think what was *so awesome* was its lack of pretense and instruction (and

Wi-Fi). As an example, we walked up to a little log cabin that had some laundry in a basket and a bar of soap. The kids got right to it, washing the laundry, and hanging it on the line. Then they discovered a rusty old push lawn mower, and Tobi spent the better part of twenty minutes mowing the grass. I watched in awe. The work was serious business, and they moved from place to place like they had a job to do, making a rope and a corn cob doll. They found a litter of kittens in the barn, who crawled all over both kids as they lounged on bales of hay. They found a snake next to an old wagon and chased each other with it.

We spent a great deal of time comparing a dugout and a shanty, debating our reasoning for both, finally deciding one needs a dugout in the winter and a shanty in the summer. There were few employees around, and even fewer guests, but somehow Tobi was taught to drive a horse and buggy and went in circles all over the grasses. I wondered what kind of insurance they had but I pushed that modern thinking away as fast as it came. We ended our day with a wagon ride out to the old schoolhouse where Laura had taught. The forty-five minutes I'd allowed became an entire day, and the highlight of our trip. We drove out of town as night fell. Charlotte pointed out Ma and Pa's grave site, asking if I wanted to stop. I declined. It was enough to know they were there.

CHAPTER 16

LOVE IN THE MARGINS

"Did you come home because I'm dying?"

It was January 1, 2016, and my mother was climbing into a hospital bed that had just been set up by a hospice nurse in the paneled family room of my parents' home. It was a common house in a common subdivision of a common suburb of Cincinnati, Ohio. The commonness of the end of their life stood out in sharp juxtaposition to the life they'd led. Like they'd downsized from a box of sixty-four crayons to a yellow number-two pencil.

"Yes. I did."

She started to cry.

My answer has haunted me for years. My younger child often asks deep and searching questions like "What was the happiest moment of your life?" or "What causes war?" In answer to the question "If you could go back in time and change one thing?" I would definitely change this answer to Mom's question. I'd spent a childhood lying to get attention. Why choose this moment to tell the unvarnished truth?

Hospice had arrived a week earlier and explained in soothing tones that Medicare would approve round-the-clock care if someone was "considered within days of death." Making sure we had that approval was essential. The money was gone before Mom was. And we still had Dad to deal with.

Mom, once she was settled into her bed, her bony hand grip-
ping the metal rail, looked at me with her piercing brown eyes and
informed me in no uncertain terms, "I'm not ready." Their cat, Ethel
from Bethel, climbed up on her and defiantly nestled in. The bed was
placed exactly where Mom's La-Z-Boy chair had resided for years, in
the same spot where, just a year before, she would have flopped down
after a long day at work and yelled to Dad in the kitchen, "Charlie,
do not put too much mayonnaise on my hamburger! And no bun."

She was always on a diet. If the situation were different, she
would love how thin she was. But she hadn't eaten in months, far
outliving the time anyone thought she'd be able to live on the TPN,
an intravenous food delivered to her via a port. TPN stands for Total
something or other. Frankly, it's too depressing to look up now. Some
things are better left in the past.

From Dad's perspective, Mom was right where she belonged. He
was sitting in his La-Z-Boy, positioned to the left of Mom's hospital
bed, in the same setup they'd occupied for years. He pointed the
remote at the TV and said, "What do you want to watch, darling?"
Only if he turned his head and looked would he notice she was in
a bed instead of her chair.

She replied, weakly, "You pick, Charlie."

He turned on Fox News, volume at 37.

"Not that."

He didn't hear her. Some blonde was talking.

She took a deeper breath. "Charlie. Not that."

He searched for the remote, which had fallen under the stacks
of newspapers in his lap.

"Hold on a second now." He found the remote and hit mute.
"What'd you say?"

"Not that. Turn on a movie."

He found *That Touch of Mink* on Turner Classics and announced, "Here we go."

"Can I get you anything, honey?" he asked. "Would you like a scrambled-egg sandwich?"

She answered sharply, as she had for months, sick of the repeated question. "No, Charlie. I can't eat."

He muted the TV again and looked over at her. "What do you mean you can't eat?"

He looked closer. "What are you doing in a bed?" She didn't answer, exhausted. He started to get agitated and bellowed: "Is somebody going to tell me what's happening here?"

The hospice nurse looked up from her clipboard, nervous, looking to see if she should answer.

I jumped in. Frank answers and managing Dad had been my job from childhood. "Dad, she has an IV that feeds her. She can't eat because of her cancer."

Mom rolled over gingerly and closed her eyes.

I explained to him, for the eighth or ninth time that day, Mom's cancer diagnosis. The surgeries. The failed attempts to keep it from spreading. I explained we'd told him over and over.

He got mad at all the same stuff. The insurance company. The doctors. Accusations flew. "Are you all keeping this from me? No one has mentioned one WORD of this to me."

I moved him into the living room and explained in detail, which had to include telling him about his dementia. Then the tears came, as they always did. "That poor kid," he said. "That poor, poor kid." He often said that. About six months earlier he'd said as we were leaving the hospital, "It should be me in here."

I agreed. He'd had diabetes since the eighties, causing toe amputations and dementia. His eating habits were legendary, especially his devotion to copious amounts of mayonnaise. He once declared, "You know, besides your mother, mayonnaise is the great love of my life."

Mom used to say when he died she was going to cremate him and put his ashes in a Hellman's jar. He would roar with laughter, saying, "Honey, put me right up there, on the mantel. I want to be able to see everything that's going on." Everyone, including him, thought he'd go first.

He looked at me like a child and said, "I know you just told me, but tell me again. Slowly. What's wrong with her?"

I started again.

My mother had neuroendocrine tumors, less formally known as zebra cancer due to its rarity. Her diagnosis came suddenly and was a shock because Mom was annoyingly healthy. She erred on the side of salads and vegetarian pizza with "light cheese." She power-walked around the mall every Saturday morning with her "walking group," an activity I was roped into when I came into town. I went mostly so I could spend time with her; she was always running to something when she wasn't working her forty-hour workweek running the surgeons' office at a major medical center.

Mom worked at her job almost to the end, dragging herself in, sick all day at work, refusing to believe she would get anything but better. And she needed to get better. She knew she had to take care of my dad as his diabetes ravaged his body and mind.

I traveled to be with her as much as I could, which ended up being a lot, and I stayed at their house. This intimate housing arrangement afforded me a unique opportunity to witness details in a way I may have missed had I lived in town.

Every morning, Mom left the newspaper on Dad's chair in the family room, opened to the Cryptogram she'd finished in the morning paper. He'd pick it up first thing and declare, "Your mother is smart as a whip!"

They often communicated through the newspaper, leaving each other notes in the margins, circling names of people and places they knew in a shorthand only they understood. Sometimes in words, but often just underlined with "!!!" inked in. Late at night Dad would cut out comics for her and leave them on her chair, thrilled when his picks made her laugh enough to earn a spot on the refrigerator. Mom and Dad kept extremely different hours and they bickered, but the proof was there. Their love was in the margins.

I was there for their last conversation, a big effort for Mom. While everyone else had left the room to give them privacy, I moved closer.

"Chuck," my mother whispered.

He leaned down. "What is it, darlin'?"

"Promise me something. This is important."

"Anything.

"Remember you have to change your pants. You get mayonnaise stains on them and they just look awful. You have a bunch of new ones in your closet. Promise me you'll wear them."

"Mary Jo, I'll try. But I can't promise."

She fell into a coma immediately afterwards and died a day and a half later. He was in the clean khakis I'd laid out for him.

For months after she died Dad would look around and say, "Where's your mother?" Again and again and again Susan, Buzz, and I had to tell him Mom died. He'd cry and re-mourn her every time, saying all the same things. Some days he'd say, "I want to ask where your mother is, but I think I don't want to know. Is that right?" On others he'd ask quietly, almost in a whisper, "Tell me something. Your mother died, didn't she?" And then he'd cry, saying, "I knew it. I didn't want to know it. But I knew it. That poor kid."

The conversations about my mom were devastating. Horrible. But sometimes, his dementia worked in his favor. My dad loved nothing more than good news, and about a month after my mom died, I got the official call that *Come From Away* was going to Broadway and I was going with it.

When my dad became overwrought about my mother dying, I'd tell him about *Come From Away*. The conversation always went like this:

"Dad. I have some incredible news. Do you want to hear it?"

"You know I do."

"I got a job. A great job. I am going to be in a brand-new Broadway show."

He'd start to laugh in the most delighted way. Every single time.

"Are you kidding me? Tell me something. Do you have a big part?"

"You know, Charles, I do. I have a big part." I always called him by his first name in times of celebration.

"Tell me what the show is about."

"Well, it's about the days on and around 9/11 when people were traveling and could not get back to the United States in airplanes." And then I would wait. On a good day he'd remember.

"I think that happened to your mother and me."

"It did. You were in Africa."

"I knew that."

"Of course you did."

"So this is a whole show about people like your mom and me, huh? Is it a musical?"

"It is. And guess what else."

"Tell me."

"I sing a lot. And it's a little bit country sounding. Remember how you always said I should be a country singer?"

"Well, I think I do remember that." Sometimes he'd sing Patsy Cline's "Crazy," and I'd sing along. Then I'd keep going.

"And I play a Texan who falls in love with a British guy and she can't stop kissing him."

More of that delighted laughter.

"This is in*credible* news, darlin'! And you're living in New York City with life by the tail. How about that?"

"How about that!"

Then, every single time, he'd get his mouth close to the phone and he'd say, in a quiet and serious dad voice, "Tell me something. Are you making good money?"

Making money was so important to him, and I knew that.

I was happy to tell him, "I am. You do not have to worry about me. And the best news is, I have Mom's ability to manage money, thank God. Not yours."

And he'd laugh again. And then he'd ask. "Does your mother know about this?"

And sometimes I'd say yes. Not just because it was the easiest way out of the conversation, but because I believed she did know. I could hear her Dr. Scholl's stopping at my bedroom door, cheering me on. "She knows, Charles. She knows."

CHAPTER 17

THE MANSION

Rental Information:

    Location: Cruise America, Fairfield, Ohio

    Vehicle Information: Size Large (30 Foot)

    Number of passengers: 3

    Departure Date: June 11, 2020

    Return Date: September 8, 2020

    Number of Nights Rented: 90

    Miles Driven: 12,298

    Total Bill: $13,518.39

Charlotte and I stood on the lot with George and his wife, Noelle. Tony, my other Cruise America buddy, was off work that day. "Tony's going to be so mad he missed you. We watched your trip on Facebook all summer," George told me, as he handed me my receipt. "It sure looked like you had a great time. You really got out there." He pointed to the receipt. "I'd have to check on this to be sure, but I am fairly certain this is the longest rental Cruise America has ever had!"

"Ever?"

"And you girls rented it at just the right time. Just after you left it seems everyone figured out that RVs were the way to go. We can't keep them in stock. And," he raised his eyebrow, "you'd never get near the price you paid. These things are renting for double."

"At least!" Noelle chimed in. "We keep getting women who are afraid to drive the RV and we've been telling them all summer about the two of you, out there driving like it's no big deal, dumping the tanks and everything!"

"Do you tell them we smashed into a hidden fire hydrant?"

George laughed. "We leave that part out. Let's see the damage." We walked over to the door side of the RV and George deemed it "fixable." As we said goodbye, he held up a black T-shirt like the one he was wearing. "We were sad to miss Martha, so give her this T-shirt for me." It was a black polyester polo-type shirt with the words "Cruise America" stamped on the right side.

"Careful what you're doing here," I said. "Martha will show up and report for work one morning."

"She really will," Charlotte added. "Seriously."

George nodded in acknowledgment. "That'd be fine, just fine."

Charlotte and I climbed back into the Honda and pulled out. It felt like driving a toddler's Barbie Jeep. "It's going to take me a while to get used to driving this thing again." I felt a little sad. "I never thought I'd like an RV but I'm really going to miss having a toilet in the car."

"And a refrigerator," Charlotte added.

We were in Cincinnati for several days, and with the RV turned in I checked out Airbnb to find a place to stay. After spending ninety nights in a two-hundred-and-fifty-square-foot RV, this listing caught my eye: "Large, private, top floor, three-bedroom in Historic Mansion. 5,000 square feet of living space is all yours!"

With two kids, two dogs, and the contents of an RV to sort through and repack, I knew this listing was the one for us.

Suddenly we had all the space we needed and then some, and then some more. The shower was a room to itself and had three shower heads in a row. At one point Tobi turned on all three shower heads and showered by running from stream to stream, singing Dua Lipa songs at the top of their lungs.

But packing to get back to New York City was a nightmare. Charlotte and I sorted everything out on the Mansion's driveway and tried to pare it down, but I was totally overwhelmed. Even if I got it to New York, where would we put all this stuff? I'd take a picture of something and send it to Martha with the question *Keep or not keep?* She responded with the word I least wanted to hear.

Dishes and cookware?

Keep

BBQ and tools?

Keep

10 ft square pop-up sunshade?

Keep

Levelers?

Keep

Elbow attachment for tanks?

Keep

Martha, how am I supposed to fit all this in the Honda?

Silence.

After a series of negative Covid-19 tests, Martha had been cleared to work once production moved into New York City to film the movie. She was working seventy-plus hours a week and would text for a minute and then suddenly disappear for hours.

"I'll take some of it," Charlotte said. "I mean, not all of it, but I'll need it for my apartment."

Now that she'd graduated, Charlotte was coming back to New York City. She was moving in with us and sharing a room with Tobi. We had plenty of room. Especially compared with the RV's square footage. Not to be one of those super-creepy moms who never wants their kids to leave home, but I was hopeful Charlotte would just stay with us . . . forever.

She gave me a brief but effective lecture about independence blah blah blah, so I said, "Well Charlotte, consider this the greatest garage sale ever. Take whatever you want!"

I rented a minivan, Charlotte packed up what she wanted from the RV, we kissed my brother Buzz and sister-in-law Maryday goodbye, peeled Tobi and Lizzy apart, and headed to New York City. We pulled into Manhattan and did exactly what Martha told us to do in one efficient text. *Put it all in storage.*

Martha's solution to everything was a storage unit.

◆ ◆ ◆

Life resumed with partial normalcy. Tobi started school virtually, Charlotte found a job, and I waited for Martha to come home. Without the constant travel I had nothing to do but make meals and think about how much I missed her. When she finally came home it was a reunion for the ages. By then Charlotte had found an apartment, taken her RV supplies, and moved out, but she still came for dinner and game night several times a week. She'd barge right into Tobi's room without knocking—something Martha and I never did because of Tobi's demand for "alone time"—and we'd hear screaming and laughing as they started to wrestle. They played video games to the end, narrating loudly. Tobi often said to Charlotte, "You're my best friend, you know." Charlotte agreed.

Midtown Manhattan took a particularly hard hit in the pandemic; with all the theaters shut down, the restaurants and hotels struggled. While other parts of New York City started to feel almost back to normal, our whole neighborhood of Midtown, nicknamed "Hell's Kitchen," remained depressed. Our friend Ellen had given Martha a mask that said *Hell's Kitchen Tough*, which Martha wore, but it felt false. We hadn't been there for the toughest times, for the sirens and sickness that had plagued the city earlier that year, but we still felt a part of the rebuild. Our building was one of the few places that continued the 7 p.m. shout-out to the front-line workers, and residents gathered nightly in a large circle in our courtyard, blowing whistles and banging pans. We'd hear it every night during dinner, serenaded by our Hell's Kitchen Tough neighbors, and we were glad to be home for it.

Having dinner at home with the kids at a normal dinner hour is something Broadway workers usually have to sacrifice because we work six days a week at odd hours and always on the weekend. The constant cooking of three meals a day wasn't my favorite, but to have all this time with my family was a silver lining in a stormy and cloud-filled year. We started a family tradition where we would each answer the following questions during dinner, one person at a time.

What was your happiest moment of the day?

What was the saddest?

What was the funniest?

What made you the maddest or most anxious?

What are you the most grateful for?

One night Tobi said, "I know this might sound awful, and I know a lot of people have been sick and died, but I am the most grateful for the pandemic. I have really loved spending all of this time together."

I took their hand and thanked them. "Me too, kid. Me, too."

We looked at Martha, whose eyes were all squinty; she was holding her breath. "You doing okay, Mar?" Tobi asked.

"I just really love you guys and I don't know how we'll ever go back to work and I think we should just move to Cincinnati and I'll drive a cement truck to support us and—"

"Yes, Mar!" Tobi yelled.

"No!" I laughed and stood up, clearing the table and breaking the mood. "Broadway is coming back, and we will have jobs. And that's that." I looked at all of them. "And Tobi will go back to school, and Charlotte, you will work as a director in theater, and we will all appreciate our lives and each other even more when we have it all back. And we will cherish this forever."

Ethel jumped up on the dinner table to make herself known.

"This is a family of survivors. We make hard times fun."

Many New Yorkers stayed in the city for the entire pandemic. We were so lucky, so privileged to be able to cobble together enough money to travel the way we did and literally run away from the city we loved so much.

◆ ◆ ◆

New York City had changed. Restaurants had closed. Streets were empty. We managed as many outdoor activities as we could, going apple-picking and seeing friends out on the street, but then it became too cold to see anyone. We walked and walked the dogs. We visited Martha's storage space. We managed mundane life things like cleaning out closets. I had surgery on my eye. Ethel is still kicking.

I Zoomed with the *Come From Away* cast twice a week. These Zooms became a lifeline for all of us. We rarely missed a chance to laugh with a group of people who were not just co-workers or friends, but family. We learned about Paul's wife having twins, we celebrated everyone's birthday, we supported each other's worries and health scares, and, mostly, we speculated when—or if—we'd ever have a job again. There were rumors, but nothing anyone could ever believe.

The Zoom calls were, as we sing in *Come From Away*, what led us out of the darkness. Before every performance of *Come From Away* we have a group circle where we chant in unison: "You are here!"

The Zoom calls were our circle. The reminder: You are here.

CHAPTER 18

A MIRACLE ON 34TH STREET

It was Martin Luther King Day 2021. We'd been back in New York for months and I'd avoided going through the piles of mail. I hate mail. Martha had made a small stack of things for me to open, and I ripped open a Macy's envelope and hit the jackpot. Star Reward coupons that were set to expire. I talked to Martha and Tobi, asking them if it was cool for me to split for a little while and head down to my favorite place in the entire world, Macy's in Herald Square.

My snobby New York friends mock me, exclaiming, "I won't set foot in there!"

I mock them right back. "Seriously? Miracle on 34th Street? Do you have a heart of stone?"

You can't get more New York than Macy's. It takes up an entire city block in the heart of Midtown. Need a bathroom? Macy's has a million of them. A good neighbor to all, Macy's is responsible for some of New York City's New Yorky-est events, like the Thanksgiving Day parade where Broadway shows perform (it's still on my bucket list, I've never done it) and the 4th of July fireworks. In the spring there is a large flower show, making the entire store smell like what I imagine the country of Holland smells like, the only difference being you can buy a Coach purse as you look at the tulips. It is as

New York as the Statue of Liberty, and my favorite place to wander when I need retail therapy. Bonus: it's close to Broadway. I can jog down there between shows, snag a duvet cover that is 50% off, add my 30%-off Star Reward coupon, making it basically free, grab some Chipotle, and jog back up to do the second show.

I could live in Macy's. I know it like the back of my hand. I'd sleep on the beds on nine, with sheets from linens on six, where I'd also grab pajamas at Intimates (skipping the designer lingerie on the left, instead heading for cozy flannels on the right). I'd grab some McDonald's on seven, which also has my favorite restroom, tucked in near the Kids Guess Collection. Starbucks is on the mezzanine. Santaland is on eight. My kids believed Santa and his reindeer lived in an apartment on the roof of Macy's Herald Square. During the holiday season, head to the ninth floor and sit on a couch (it's the furniture floor and the top floor). If you're very quiet, you can hear the reindeer hooves as they stomp in the cold.

When I was twenty-four years old, I worked at a restaurant on the mezzanine of Macy's Herald Square. It overlooked the famous ground-level shopping floor. It was Macy's most elegant restaurant, complete with white tablecloths. I'd applied for a job as an elf in Santaland, but because I had waitress experience I ended up in Cafe L'Etoile. My hilarious friend Stefanie got the elf job. I would visit her on my lunch break and find her laughing with the kids, "I'm a Jewish elf named Matzoh Ball!"

Cafe L'Etoile was more serious. My job was to serve Cobb salads and iced tea to the Ladies Who Lunched (and shopped). I got the job to pay off the large debt I had incurred in college. Some of that debt was from a student loan, but most of it was simply from money mismanagement. I started getting credit card applications in the mail at the end of my senior year. My parents' finances were falling apart at the same time, so I'd been cut loose financially. I took cash advances on all the cards and ignored the bills as they rolled in. By fall of 1992, I was thousands of dollars in debt, but slowly chipping away at it. I'd handed over all my financials to my then-boyfriend, who had made it clear that he would not marry me unless I paid off this debt. He said he would not (and could not) help me with money, but he would manage the money I made and pay off the bills for me. The more I smiled and schmoozed at Cafe L'Etoile, the better my tips, and the closer I was to an engagement ring. I walked into Macy's every day with high hopes and walked out with a pocket full of cash. As much as I wanted to be goofing around in Santaland, I was pulling in probably three times more cash than Elf Matzoh Ball.

While at Cafe L'Etoile, I received two critical phone calls, which came in on the kitchen phone. One, on December 7th, 1992, was from my brother Buzz, telling me my sister Susan had had a baby girl. December 7th was also my 25th birthday, and I was so excited I ran to the seventh floor and bought every pink baby outfit I could afford; my only splurge while working there. Three days later, on December 10th, I got the call on the kitchen phone that I had an audition for *Les Miserables*, a phone call that changed the trajectory of my career. I got the job, hugged my co-workers goodbye, and flew to Los Angeles, where I joined the National Touring Company. My final days at Cafe L'Etoile had paid off my debt. I joined *Les Miserables*, which paid more money than any job I'd ever had, debt-free. I was engaged thirteen months later, and we registered at—you guessed it—Macy's.

In 2008, around the time Tobi was born, my parents, who had invested all of their money and their house on a wooden decking invention by my dad, went bankrupt. Buzzy and Susan and I were heartsick for them, but the invention, called Honey Deck, was a great one. It had just been picked up by Home Depot, but during its first weekend on shelves in a small test market in Florida, Florida was hit by a hurricane. People rushed past the displays of Honey Deck to buy plywood and supplies to board up their home, and all of Honey Deck's dreams were dashed. My mom made a deal with the government that she'd work to pay off the money in exchange for decimated credit. Mom asked me if she could open a Macy's card in my name so she could buy Christmas presents for the kids, and she went on to pay off every bill on time, raising my credit score at a time when hers was zero. She'd call as she was shopping in her local Macy's on Beechmont Avenue and say, "I'm thinking of you! I have my coupons!" When she would visit New York, she'd take Charlotte and Tobi to Macy's and buy them back-to-school shoes and lunch, all on that same card.

January 6th is the anniversary of my mom's death, and the whole month is historically tough for me. January 2021 marked the five-year anniversary of her death, the one-year anniversary of the first cases of Covid-19 in the United States, and ten months since Broadway had shut down. I was blue, so I walked the cold and empty streets down to Macy's, alone, needing something—something familiar and warm. Some retail therapy. As I'd learned over the years, Martha did laundry to settle down and I browsed in Macy's. As I walked, I reflected on what had happened in the *Come From Away* Zoom call the night before. There was a rumor that our show was going to be filmed, much like *Diana* had been. I was having a hard time believing it.

I am historically an optimist, but in the last year my profession had been decimated and so too had my optimism. In October we'd learned Broadway was closed until at least June, but everyone said it would be longer, and I'd allowed myself to begin believing it.

Financially we were hanging in, many thanks to all who fought for unemployment and stimulus packages, but (speaking for myself) I just wanted to work. Nothing could compare with the feeling of being able to pay for everything myself, a feeling I had not had enough of in my life and relished. Now I'd really started to wonder: would shows ever come back?

I walked into Macy's that night wishing I could call Mom. I wanted to apologize for complaining about how much she worked, especially as she was battling cancer. I could not, at the time, conceive why a person would continue to drag themselves to work like that. Now, in the pandemic, I felt a deep connection to her need to work. If she stopped working, she was no longer Capable Mary Jo who zoomed around the office, planning everything; she became a woman dying of cancer. Me without a job and no Broadway to strive toward meant I was an under-skilled, unemployed rudderless ship. Work was a huge part of my mother's identity. And it was a huge part of my identity, too.

I decided to soothe myself in the intimate apparel section. Mom always bought me underwear for Christmas, and I needed some, the main excuse for my Macy's trip. I stopped and bought a coffee on the Mezzanine, near where the old Cafe L'Etoile had been, noting the space now housed scarves and hats. I took the wooden elevators to the seventh floor and meandered through the sales racks. Maybe some pajamas, too, if I could find a deal. The store was empty. I worried it would close, too, or even worse, be bought out by Amazon and become a warehouse. Even Macy's wasn't helping my woes.

My phone dinged and my watch buzzed. I had an email. I put down the package of Jockeys I was holding at the price check and opened my phone to this email from one of our lead producers, Sue:

Dear all,

We hope that you are all well and continuing to stay safe during these tumultuous times.

We know there have been some rumors flying around about a live capture, and this email is to confirm those rumors! Entertainment One, the company that holds the film rights, has done a "pandemic pivot" and is now committed to filming a live capture of our Broadway production this spring. After much discussion of dates, most of which has been driven by the pandemic, we have settled on filming the show during the week of May 10th, 2021. While we do not have a firm start date, given the vagaries of quarantine, amount of rehearsal etc., we are asking you to put a hold on the time period from April 5 to May 16th. Now that the cat is officially out of the bag with all of you, Alchemy will be reaching out to the unions, your agents, and the rest of the company. We expect a lot of information will start rolling out very soon.

I sat down, right next to the price checker, and burst into tears.

I called a million people as I walked around the store, still holding the Jockey underwear. I ran home, packages under my arm, the cast recording of *Come From Away* playing in my earbuds. I hadn't been able to listen to anything related to the show since the shutdown, worried it could spiral me into a depression too deep to bear. But now, it was different. I had to get ready! I hadn't done a thing since March 12th, 2020. I needed to get strong again, to sing, to go on a diet, to whiten my teeth. Martha enjoyed how girlie-girl I became as I prepped. I'd come out of the bathroom with yet another facemask on and she'd say, "I like all this movie star stuff." Me too. I couldn't wait.

I packed up my bags, kissed my people goodbye, so grateful that Tobi was about to have fun, too; they would be starting in-person school while I was gone. It was spring, and it felt like it. The vaccine rollout was happening as the flowers bloomed. I managed to squeeze in my vaccine just before shooting—as did most people on the set—making my experience less worrisome than Martha's had been. No amount of facemasks or daily testing could dilute the sheer joy of this company of people being together again. It was everything and more.

Here is what I finally allowed myself to believe: the film would play on Apple+ TV. The show would reopen on Broadway. If my life were a golf ball, it would be rolling back toward the center. In a true full circle moment, days before we reopened on Broadway, we appeared on *Good Morning America*. We'd shut Broadway down with them, and we opened it up with them, this time performing outside in the middle of Times Square, surrounded by the bright neon lights of Broadway. Back in business.

Back in an early Zoom call, Kenny, one of the show's lead producers, told us, "We will reopen the show when we can reopen it with hugs and full houses. We will not reopen in fear." My dad couldn't have said it better. I thought of my mom, of one of the last things she'd said to me: "Go be my happy girl."

If you are somewhere in the middle of nowhere, don't doubt. Drive.

CHAPTER 19

BROADWAY'S REVIVAL

On September 21st, 2021, after 559 days and 630 performances missed, the curtain rose on *Come From Away* at the Schoenfeld Theater on W. 45th Street. It was an outstanding night, even in an industry that routinely turns out outstanding nights. There were five standing ovations. There was a fifteen-minute standing ovation at the end of the show. I was tasked with taking a selfie of the entire cast, crew, band, and audience that night. I stood on a table and documented the momentous occasion in a picture, and if you look closely, you'll see our pandemic buddies Buzz, Maryday, and

Maryday's mom, Pat, who drove up from Cincinnati to share the start of this moment. This picture of eleven hunded ecstatic faces welcomes back not just our show, but live theater in New York. Please support live theater. We need you.

But this wasn't our first post-pandemic public appearance.

On September 10th, 2021, *Good Morning America* invited the cast of *Come From Away* back to perform on the show as participants in their "Broadway is Back" series. Considering our last public performance as a group was on *Good Morning America* on March 12, 2020, the day of the shutdown, it held special meaning for all of us. Even host Michael Strahan pointed out, "*Come From Away* was here the day Broadway shut down, and now they are here to bring us back." We performed outdoors in the middle of Times Square. An electrifying, full-circle moment.

Many things have changed on Broadway. Patrons and performers must be vaccinated. There are masks, and there are Covid Safety Officers (Charlotte is one, in fact). But it's not just the pandemic that has changed Broadway. The murder of George Floyd, the Black Lives Matter marches around the world, and the voices chanting for change in our industry have led to the small but growing swells of a sea change. Stories *must* be equitably told. Actors, designers, musicians, crew, and creators must be diverse and show an accurate snapshot of the world as it is today, not the world frozen in time in the 1950s. We all must rise up. I cannot write a book about this time on Broadway without including the movement that has so sharply formed our new normal.

Since I grew up in a white world of privilege, I do not feel my voice is the right voice to amplify this subject. I asked my dear friend and dressing roommate, Q. Smith, who plays Hannah in *Come From*

Away, if she might be willing to donate her time and point of view to this book.

◆ ◆ ◆

sw: Q., I want to say thank you, first and foremost, for agreeing to share your feelings and knowledge. As you know when I asked you to do this, I wanted to lean into this topic and garner a greater understanding rather than leaning out because I don't feel worthy. My belief is that much can change by one-on-one conversations just like this. Since this is a movement, I want to talk about that. Movement means changing places, going from one to the next. So, these are my questions about how diversity and equity resonate with you.

What was it like before the shutdown? What was not working?

qs: Before the shutdown I had the sense that people of color had become resigned to the idea that they would always feel marginalized. In America, we had gotten used to the idea that we had to work twice as hard, scream twice as loud, run twice as fast just to *be* seen. In the performing arts, we got used to the idea that we would always play second fiddle or be used as props to service the fully developed storylines of our white counterparts. And there was always this feeling that we should be "grateful" to have the token "person of color" role in a show. Before the shutdown I think people of color were always groomed to feel or be grateful for the very little we were being given or allowed to have.

Before the shutdown, the tragic death of George Floyd, and the civil unrest that followed, there were a lot of unspoken issues, especially surrounding race, privilege, and equality that people were not having, even in their closest circles. Conversations on those topics were either tiptoed around or avoided altogether. I've felt that it's usually the marginalized person that has to suppress their urge to talk about these things, scream out "hey what about me!?" for the sake of everyone else's comfortability. I've witnessed a lot of that before the shutdown.

But after the shutdown . . . I just think everyone was tired. Black people, and the like minded, were just fed up with accepting anything that looked like "less than." Done with injustices, done with racism, done with absolving others for their own benefit, done holding our tongues. Just done! We were *going* to have these conversations. We were *going* to say our piece, speak our grievances, and fight for our rights. Period.

sw: What is it like now going back? Does it feel any different?

as: I definitely feel like now, because of what we all went through as a country, BIPOC, and other marginalized artists, are way more confident about making their voices heard and making sure we are seen. It is much easier to hold the industry accountable when you don't feel like you are out there on a limb by yourself. What came out of the last 18 months was a solidarity that we can do better and we must do better. Doors will swing open wider because there is this sense in the air like "yeah, this has always been an issue. It's time to change it." And that's both in this country and in this industry.

It feels a bit different coming back, but for all the right reasons. Like the line from our show says, "We all look the same, but we're different than before." I had a lot of joy coming back and that's in part to our CFA family communicating to us all that they were doing the work necessary to make sure this would be a safe place to come back to. Our show is unique in that the very essence of it is in a lot of ways a model to what we are striving for outside of this theater. I think every single person in the Schoenfeld Theatre gets that and is committed to living it both on- and offstage.

sw: What is your ideal for the future? Do you believe it can happen?

as: My ideal future includes a world where I can raise my son to believe that there are truly no limits on him. To me, that is a world where everyone feels welcomed, included, and safe to express themselves culturally and artistically. I want to see more art that changes ideals. I want to see boundaries pushed and a lot more people willing to get into "good trouble." I want each and every one of us to be challenged to rise to our best selves.

And, it can happen. It is already beginning.

sw: You had a son in January of 2020, and you lost your father in late 2019. How will your son's life differ from your dad's?

as: The irony of this question is that if my son was in his teens now, his world and how it treats black men would look very similar to the world my dad encountered during his teens. That's scary. It's like with every generation we take steps forward, but then somehow take just as many steps back. But my son is almost two so there is time.

My dad rose above hatred, and I'll always admire him for that. My dad loved everyone, despite what they may have said or done to him. My prayer for my son is that he won't have to be judged or lynched because he wears a hoodie at night or that he won't be passed over for a job he's qualified for, or teased, or spit on, or ever feel threatened all because of his beautiful black skin. I truly believe that because of my father, and people like my father, Caleb will grow up in love and have all the opportunities everyone else is allowed to have. He will be free to be his authentic beautiful Black self. This is the hope for us all.

CHAPTER 20

POSITIVE ENDINGS

And just like that, on December 21, 2021, I tested positive for Covid. The Omicron variant showed up with a point to prove, infecting everyone in its wake.

My friend Dona, whom I called right after I found out, bellowed, "Sharon! And Jesus wept!" Coming from anyone else that might sound dramatic and overly religious, but said in Dona's thick Jamaican accent and followed by her enormous laugh, it was utterly perfect.

She said it again. "And Jesus wept! Did you turn in that book yet? Eh? Because you'll have to put this in there, you know. You can't leave all those people believing you ran around in a van avoiding this whole disease with your superpowers. You have to tell them! It got you!" She then turned practical, "You got your boost? Yes? You'll be fine. Two shots and the boost and you'll be okay. I heard that on TV this morning." Then, thinking of herself, she added, "I won't be seeing you for two weeks, thank you very much. Merry Christmas and Happy New Year."

We were all fine—me, Martha, and Tobi, who all tested positive within days of each other. Although "fine" in our case was still sick. But being sick without fear of ending up on a ventilator is a very different thing, and for that we are grateful, grateful, grateful. Our Covid Christmas looked a lot like the beginning of the pandemic. I made bread and soup, we ate too much, we binge-watched TV, and I took everyone's temperature a thousand times a day. We sprayed Charlotte's Christmas presents with Lysol and left them outside our door, opening them with her later on FaceTime

Because of widespread infections, Broadway shows, including mine, stopped performances temporarily as the virus pummeled Broadway workers during the lucrative Christmas holiday weeks. Those same shows then reopened with determined and talented understudies, standbys, and swings; some of whom hadn't done the shows they were stepping into for years or, in some cases, at all. Many times, those workers became infected, and the the shows suspended performances again to allow everyone to recover. *The Radio City Christmas Spectacular* cancelled its run two weeks early after a rumored fifty performers and crew members became infected. A few shows closed temporarily, hopeful they will return when the infection rate goes down. Some shows, like Martha's show *Diana*, will not reopen. Other shows temporarily paused. *Come From Away*'s company in Toronto closed, a terrible shock to all of them. They were the last company of *Come From Away* to reopen after the pandemic and had only performed seven shows when their Covid-19 outbreak, along with new capacity limitations in Canada (and a lack of government funding), ultimately closed their show for good.

All of these people, these "The show must go on" people, who were sidelined for so long while others worked from home, had their commitment to this business and its future tested once again by the variant in late 2021. I have friends who have left the business forever and even more who have moved out of New York City in search of an easier life and some fresh air. But Broadway is open, and for many people New York is our forever home. I am part of the hopeful crowd. The minute I was better and through quarantine, I sprang into action, seeing three shows in twenty-four hours, desperate to cheer on and give money to the shows that were open. *Come From Away* is open on Broadway, and I still have my job. Grateful, grateful, grateful.

It's hard to stay positive in these times, and I'd be lying if I said that the pandemic had not changed some of the hardwiring in my brain. I find I am weary of optimism. I read something recently, a social media post from a friend condoning what they called "toxic positivity."

Toxic positivity.

Huh.

I think I have been guilty of that. I think I want everything to be happy at any cost. Or for everything to *mean* something. Or for there to be a *lesson learned*.

But maybe all I really know, for sure, is that sometimes you can see something coming at you. Or you can feel it. And I would encourage you to honor that feeling, and look at it, and weigh it, and ask yourself, "Is there anything I can do to make this manageable? Can I make it (dare I say it) a little more fun?"

Because you can't always control it.

But you might be able to make some bread if you have flour and yeast.

Or you might be able to still have Christmas presents if you decided to do a power shop at Macy's just days before you tested positive . . . just in case . . .

Or you might be able to see the world from an RV if you book that thing early enough.

THE MANY THANKS

Thank you, Martha, for allowing me to share our epic journey. Thank you, Charlotte and Tobi, for all the things that you do and endure and enjoy. My heart beats for you.

Thank you to my *Come From Away* family around the globe, especially to Sue Frost, Randy Adams, and Kenny and Marleen Alhadaff, who are the best producers on Broadway. Also thank you to David Hein and Irene Sankoff for loaning me the title of "Somewhere in the Middle of Nowhere," which is a song title in the show and a perfect subtitle for this book. Thank you to their daughter, Molly, who is my favorite kid to turn into a cat. Thank you to Chris Ashley for being a brilliant creative steward, to Kelly Devine who pushed us all to be our best, and to Ian Eisendrath for being our musical genius and pandemic driveway host. To Rachel Hoffman for being a great and loving casting director who brought me back from showbiz purgatory.

Thank you to everyone who hosted us in their parking lot, driveway, or yard. We made a weird request and you not only accepted us, but you hosted us with humor and grace: the La Jolla Playhouse, Matt and Jill Chesse, Linda and Paul Della Pelle, Larry, Laurie and Bryan Baldwin, Jean and Dan Dinaburg, the Seattle Repertory Theatre, Becky and Kim Pittenger, Ian and Charlie Eisendrath, Linda Balgord and Andrew Fenton, and Pat Van Over.

Thank you to Cruise America, and specifically my buddies George and Noelle Armour and Tony Fessel. Thank you to everyone who followed us on our journey on social media, it was a blast hearing from you. Thank you to the rangers in the state and national parks who kept us all safe. Thank you to the Covid testers and doctors and nurses who vaccinated everyone. Thank you to the entire health industry for stepping up in a time that is so out of this world. Our hearts are with everyone who still suffers from the effects of Covid, particularly to the many, many families who have lost loved ones. We honor those we lost.

Thank you to Lisa Queen, who believed in me and helped me at every turn.

Thank you to Buzz and Maryday and Elizabeth and Gwendolyn Wheatley, as well as Pat Van Over, for being our pandemic bubble members. Let's bubble forever. To my sister Susan and my brother-in-law Tony, to my aunts Jean, Judy, Barbara, and Nancy. To my cousins. To my uncle Bill. To everyone who lent us gear when we arrived in Cincinnati in March 2020 with very little in our car and an empty house to live in. Thank you to my dear friend Lisa Zeitz, who is my soul sister forever. Thank you to Jane Orans and everyone at Quisisana Resort in Maine, for hosting a creative world in the pines where I could meet so many of my closest friends. Thank you to Rob Meffe.

To Michele Mascari, Kathy Wade, and Cathy Creason, three English teachers who spent a great deal of time editing this book. We lost Creason before this book was published, but she's cheering on every page. To John Wescott, who died just before we shot the *Come From Away* movie, leaving a giant hole in my heart.

To Josh Krigman and the Writer's Rock in New York City. This book would *not* have happened with you. No way. You were my left arm, my right arm, my gas in the engine. I cannot thank you enough. What a beautiful space you've created for writers.

To Ethel, Sparky, Desi, and our late, great Dot. Thank you to our four-legged friends. Your companionship was needed more than ever.

To my brothers and sisters/castmates at *Come From Away*. I love you all. And not in a gross showbiz, fake kind of way, but in a serious, if-you-need-me-I-will-drop-anything-and-everything kind of way. Family forever. To the *Come From Away* kids, some born before we met, and those who have joined us. To our dressers (I'm looking at you, Allie), to our designers. To our rocking band and our crew. To the front-of-house staff and the production crew. To our press department. To all of those involved in making the Schoenfeld Theater our home again. Thank you to our Covid Safety Managers for making our home safe.

And finally, to my mom and dad. My Chuck and MJ. Charlie and Mary Jo.

This book was not about you when I started it, but there you were. Right there. Ready for me and refusing to be ignored. How could I tell this tale without you? Thank you for guiding my way and teaching me to do it with a bit of fear and a ton of fun. I raise you both up (and I'll see you there). Cheers.

ABOUT THE AUTHOR

SHARON WHEATLEY is a Broadway actress, a writer, an educator, and a mom.

Sharon currently appears nightly as Diane and others, roles she originated, in the musical *Come From Away* on Broadway. Playing at the Schoenfeld Theater, it opened on March 12, 2017, to critical acclaim; it is a *New York Times* "Critic's Pick" and a Tony© Award Winner. Sharon's performance of Diane can be seen in the Apple+ TV film version of *Come From Away* and heard on the original cast recording.

Sharon has enjoyed many years in New York City as a professional actress. Her Broadway credits include her current role in *Come From Away* (Diane and others, original cast), *Avenue Q* (Kate Monster/ Lucy T. Slut, Mrs. T. Yellow Bear standby), the final company of *Cats* as it finished its record-breaking run at the Winter Garden Theater (Jennyanydots, The Gumbie Cat), *Les Miserables* (Cosette and Eponine understudy), and *The Phantom of the Opera* (Madam Firman). Sharon holds the distinction of being the only female actor to appear in all three of these Broadway blockbusters on Broadway. She has also toured nationally and internationally with *Les Misérables*, *The Phantom of the Opera*, and *The Sound of Music*, and also originated *Avenue Q* at the Wynn Casino and Resort in Las Vegas (Mrs. T/Yellow Bear/Kate and Lucy). Her other film credits include *Gods Behaving Badly*. On TV, she has been seen as "Mary Jo" in *My Life Is a Lifetime Movie*.

In addition to her Broadway career, Sharon is a featured soloist around the country with symphony orchestras, including the New Jersey Symphony, Detroit, Seattle, Portland, Naples, Milwaukee, Omaha, and Oklahoma City.

As a writer, Sharon has a nationally published memoir, *'Til the Fat Girl Sings (Adams Media with Simon and Schuster)*, which follows the trials and tribulations of being an overweight midwestern kid with giant Broadway dreams. Readers of all ages deeply relate to Sharon's story about an underdog on a mission to prove that talent and perseverance win out.

As a blogger, Sharon is best known for *SMASH FACT OR FICTION?* an episode-by-episode run through of what is fact and what is fiction in NBC's TV show *Smash*. This blog, written with love and fun, was written up in *Marie Claire* and named as "highbrow and brilliant" in *New York Magazine*'s "Approval Matrix," as well as appearing in various newspapers around the country.

Additionally, Sharon wrote nationally for Weight Watchers for many years and had a loyal following on her episodic story blog, My Own Space.

Sharon also wrote for actress Kristin Chenoweth, including sketches for her US and Australia tours, sketches for the Hollywood Bowl, and other concerts around the country. A favorite was co-writing a parody of the song "Popular" for Kristin to sing on *The Tonight Show*, which aired on July 30th, 2013, and went on to be replayed by news outlets around the world. Sharon also produced, directed, and co-wrote *Avenue Zoo*, a 30-minute original musical written for the Bronx Zoo WCS. It ran for four months at the Bronx Zoo in 2016 and 2012, and was rewritten and performed at the Houston Zoo for four months in the summer of 2013. *Avenue Zoo* was written up in the September 2013 issue of *American Theatre Magazine*.

Sharon is a native of Cincinnati, Ohio, where she attended the renowned musical theater program at University of Cincinnati's College Conservatory of Music. In 2006 Sharon received the CCM Musical Theater Young Alumnae Award.

She runs musical theater workshops for aspiring actors at both the college and high school level. Sharon served on the advisory board of Rosie's Theater Kids, was an elected member of Actors Equity Association's National Council, and served as a voter for the Tony Awards for 8 years.

As an educator, Sharon loved teaching at the renowned Professional Performing Arts High School in New York City for several years, where she focused on auditioning for college theater programs and as an overall college preparation and selection advisor. Her talented students were accepted to major theater programs across the county.

Sharon is available to coach in person and online. She especially enjoys "Skyping in" to high school and college classes around the country to give masterclasses about careers in show business, do a Q&A on *Come From Away*, or speak with English classes who are studying and writing memoirs.

Sharon is the proud mother of Charlotte and Tobi Meffe. She wrote a parenting column for *Equity News*, the Actors' Equity Association newspaper which attracted the attention of *the New York Times*, and they featured Sharon and her kids in a story and video about a Broadway Childcare project with the Actors' Chapel. Sharon is married to Broadway stage manager Martha Donaldson. Their journey was written up in the "Styles" section of the Sunday *New York Times*.